CRYSTAL CLEAR

CRYSTAL CLEAR

CHANGE YOUR ENERGY, HEAL YOUR LIFE

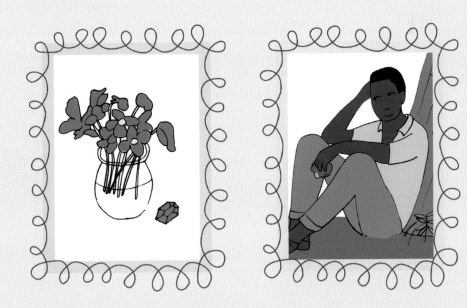

GOLNAZ ALIBAGI

CICO BOOKS
LONDON NEW YORK

To my three favorite people in the world: my mum, dad, and sister who I love with all my heart.

This hardback edition published in 2018 by CICO Books
an imprint of Ryland Peters & Small Ltd
20–21 Jockey's Fields   341 E 116th St
London WC1R 4BW   New York, NY 10029

www.rylandpeters.com

First published in 2014 as *The Essential Guide to Crystals*

10 9 8 7 6 5 4 3 2 1

Text © Golnaz Alibagi 2014, 2018
Design, illustration, and photography © CICO Books
2014, 2018

A CIP catalog record for this book is available from the
Library of Congress and the British Library.

ISBN: 978-1-78249-657-1

Printed in China

Editor: Marion Paull
Designer: Emily Breen
Illustrator: Rosie Scott
Photographers: Geoff Dann and Roy Palmer

Acknowledgments

First and foremost, I'd like to thank my beautiful little
sister, best friend and favorite person in the world
Mahsa, who—like the moon she was named after—
has always brought light into my darkest moments,
and supported me more than anyone during the
writing of this book. I'd also like to thank my amazing
mum and dad, who came to Britain with nothing and
still gave me and my little sister the best childhoods
we could have hoped for; thank you for never giving
up on me, and showing me the true meaning of
unconditional love.

I'd also like to thank CICO, and the amazing
Cindy Richards and Lauren Mulholland, for taking a
chance on me, and helping me turn my dream into a
reality; thank you for making the reality of my dream
even more wonderful than I'd imagined it would be.

I'm also very blessed to have many, many close
friends (they know who they are!), and would like to
thank them for celebrating my happiness with me,
and cheering me on every step of the way.

I'd also like to thank the wonderful writers—
particularly Judy Hall, Cassandra Eason, Phillip Permutt
and Mary Lambert—whose books have inspired me
so greatly, and who I've learnt so much from.

And last but not least, I'd like to thank you, dear
reader, for believing in me enough to pick up this
book, and loving yourself (and my words) enough to
read it to the last page.

Contents

CHIASTOLITE

DANBURITE

GOLDEN CALCITE

STICHTITE

ANGELITE

CHRYSOBERYL

HEMIMORPHITE

SERPENTINE

Introduction

Hello and welcome to your essential, no-fuss guide to attracting everything you've ever wanted using **crystals**. Whether you're hoping to attract your dream partner, job, or home, wish to maximize your bank balance, career success, or natural beauty (yes, really!), or simply want to fall in love with yourself and life again there's a gem for you. Simply look up what you're after and find your **gem-scription**.

Of course, in today's busy world, with children, jobs, and social engagements to keep up with, it can be hard to find the time, money, or energy for long-winded rituals. I've found the quickest and easiest rituals for you to try. Nothing in this book will take you longer than

15 minutes and, better still, most of the tips involve nothing more than wearing one of the **gems** around your neck (and let's face it, who doesn't love an excuse to splash out on some jewelry?)

But be warned: this book will **change your life**. Prepare for the start of a truly breath-taking adventure that will lead you straight to your **happily ever after.**

My Crystal Journey

Before we start our journey together, I'd like to tell you a bit about how my love affair with crystals began, and how it's changed my life (as I hope this book will change yours.)

Crystals first caught my eye when I watched the movie *Breakfast at Tiffany's* as a little girl, and saw my first diamond. It was love at first sight and I knew it was true love when I started writing a monthly crystal column for a spiritual magazine, and quickly found myself experiencing all the symptoms of love-sickness: I began thinking, talking, and dreaming about crystals constantly, I felt like I was on cloud nine whenever I was writing about them, and was so captivated by their exquisite beauty that every column felt like the first column. I was smitten.

Uncovering the Past

It wasn't until I had a past life reading, and received a life-changing message from myself as a little girl in a previous life, that I realized I was destined to fall in love with crystals. Let me explain.

During a past life reading, you are put into a deep hypnosis, and taken back to a previous lifetime. As I closed my eyes, and listened to the therapist's calming voice, I saw an image of myself as a little girl from a very poor family in nineteenth-century Paris. I was working on a market stall with my father, who I loved dearly (as I do in this life.)

Each morning, as I helped my father set up his stall, I'd admire the beautiful crystals sold by a gem trader nearby. One day, as he was setting up his stand, he dropped one. I picked it up and returned it to him. Touched by my honesty and kindness (I was from a poor family after all, and could have kept the crystal for myself), he let me keep it as a thank you.

I felt like a princess, and would spend hours playing with, stroking, and speaking to the gem each night as though it was a tiny animal or doll. The last thing I remember is the little girl's voice saying: "Write your crystal book Naz, please write your crystal book; don't leave the world with your crystal book still inside you." I sent my idea to the publisher the next day.

The Power of Crystals

When I first started writing this book I wanted to help you heal, not realizing I'd heal myself in the process. As I wrote about the gems to help you sow, water, and harvest the seeds of romance, friendship, domestic bliss, career success and, most importantly, self-love, I grew a garden myself. I found my soul mate (this book), weeded out the bad seeds in my friendship circle and planted new ones, and became closer to my family than ever. Any time I started doubting myself, I'd stumble upon a new crystal book, mythology, or inspiring quotation I'd never seen before.

The day I finished my last chapter, I felt like I'd lost a dear friend, only to bump into my new neighbor for the first time. Her name is Jade (the stone of friendship.)

So, dear reader, as we begin our truly magical adventure together, I hope the words in this book bring you as much joy, happiness, and hope as they've brought me, and give you the courage to find, follow, and fulfil your "crystal book"—your dream—too.

MORGANITE

Getting Started with Crystals

Before we start our journey together it's important to make the right preparations so that your crystals will be perfectly attuned to you and super-charged with healing energy. It's easy to look after your gems and, with just a little bit of time and attention, your crystals will work with you for many years, growing in power over time. As your crystal collection grows, you may find that you go through phases when some gems don't feel like a good match for you any longer. This is perfectly natural. Some gems are destined to be our lifelong companions, while others will only be with us for a short time. There may even be some crystals that we form on-off relationships with! Here's a quick guide to help you prepare for our exciting adventure.

Choosing the Right
Crystal

This is very much like packing for a holiday; certain outfits (a.k.a. gems) will suit particular occasions, and what might work for someone else may not be right for you. Here are a few tips to help you find the right one:

1

Look up your dilemma, and see which of the suggested gems you're instantly drawn to.

2

Hold this book in your hands, focus on your dilemma, and ask the gems for guidance. Open it randomly, and the first crystal you notice will lead you to the answer.

3

Spread a few gems on a table (or go to a crystal shop) and hover your hands over the gemstones. Ask them for help, and you'll soon notice your hands naturally gravitate towards one (or feel a warm sensation over it). You can also do this by opening this book on a specific chapter, and holding your hands over the page.

AMETHYST

Cleansing a Crystal

Once you've found the right gem, you'll need to cleanse it regularly (as you would an outfit) to clear any nasty stains (a.k.a. negative energy) from the past.

Generally speaking, you should have a "laundry day" once a month, or after any ritual you've completed. Make it fun by dedicating a whole day or afternoon to it, and use the power of the elements to help you.

You can either pick the one you're most drawn to, go for the element associated with your star sign, or rotate them depending on the season (ie. water for winter, fire for summer).

Water

Hold your crystal under running water for a few minutes, and leave it to dry naturally. (Note: some gems are water-soluble so avoid this method if yours isn't water-friendly. If your gem is porous or has a high metal content, don't cleanse it using water; use one of the other methods described below.)

Earth

Bury your crystal in some soil (either in your garden, or a plant pot) and leave it there for 24 hours. You can also do this on a full moon, and leave it there until a new one.

Fire

Light some incense, and waft its smoke over your gemstone for five minutes. Scents that work particularly well are sage, frankincense, sandalwood, juniper, pine, and rose. Make sure that your crystal does not get too hot or it will crack.

Air

Leave your crystal under the light of a full or new moon overnight, or under sunlight for a few hours. (Note: some crystals fade or catch fire in the sun, so try a different method unless you're absolutely certain. Crystals that shouldn't be cleansed using this method include amethyst, smoky quartz, and chrysocolla.)

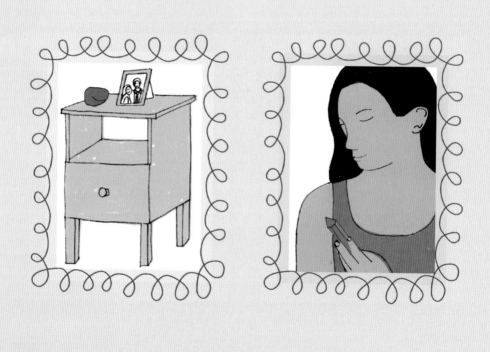

Chapter 1
Love & Romance

Tapping into the
Love Energy of Crystals

Crystals have been used to attract, nurture, and rekindle true love and romance for centuries. Whether you're trying to find your perfect partner, renew a lost love affair, or spice up an existing relationship, there's a gem for you.

While these crystals might not magically manifest your dream mate, or transform your relationship overnight, they will help you to dismantle any barriers preventing you from wholeheartedly sharing your love with another, and having the fabulous romantic life you deserve. Before we get down to the nitty gritty though, let's look at some of the best gems for romance.

Generally speaking, the pink crystals, particularly **Rose Quartz**, **Rhodochrosite**, and **Rhodonite**, are best for attracting romance. The **Rose Quartz** has been popular throughout history and has been given as a love charm since the Middle Ages right through to the present day. Simply holding one of these pastel pink gems by your chest, wearing one around your neck, or placing one beneath your pillow will gently encourage your heart to open like the petals on a beautiful rose, and inspire you to fall in love with the most important and wonderful person of all—you. Once you've done this, you'll be ready to open your heart to someone special.

The green gems, such as **Emerald**, **Green Tourmaline**, and **Green Aventurine**, are also great for matters of the heart, and will help you nurture and deepen your relationships with others and with yourself. **Emerald** in particular is considered a stone of insight and it will help you to trust yourself and know whether or not a relationship is right for you.

EMERALD

RED GARNET

GREEN AVENTURINE

Then, of course, those wonderful red stones, such as **Ruby**, **Red Garnet**, and **Red Zircon**, are fabulous for keeping things super-hot between you and your partner. The **Garnet** has been linked to love since ancient times. The name comes from the Latin word "granatus," which is part of the word "Punica Granatum," meaning pomegranate, a fruit with red seeds that are similar in shape and size to **Garnet** crystals. The pomegranate, and by extension, the **Garnet** are associated with gifts of love and eternity thanks to their links with the story of the goddess Persephone. The god of the underworld, Hades, captured this beautiful young goddess. He eventually agreed to release her but, because she had eaten six pomegranate seeds while in the underworld, she had to return there for six months every year. The seeds came to symbolize the concept of returning love.

So whether you're single or in a relationship, new to crystals, or an absolute pro, prepare for the start of a truly wonderful chapter (both literally and metaphorically) in your romantic life by trying these super-simple tips to help you find, catch, and keep your perfect match.

RHODOCHROSITE

RHODONITE

RUBY

GREEN TOURMALINE

ROSE QUARTZ

Find your soulmate, transform your relationship, and learn to love yourself...

Your Crystal Tips for Love

PEARL

CELESTITE

GOLDEN CALCITE

LAPIS LAZULI

AMBER

IMPERIAL TOPAZ

SUNSTONE

Accepting love Prepare yourself to be romance-ready by holding a Honey Opal by your heart. The gem will clear away any negative beliefs that are preventing you from accepting love, such as unworthiness, doubt, or fear, and prepare you to catch Cupid's arrow. **Alternative gemstones:** Rhodochrosite, Pearl, Celestite.

Anger toward a partner Turn your relationship from testy to zesty by placing a Rhodonite crystal beside a photo of your partner to diffuse the tension between you, and ensure the only fireworks you create together are in the bedroom. **Alternative gemstones:** Golden Calcite, Pink Carnelian, Lapis Lazuli.

Attracting a new partner Boost your sex appeal by placing a piece of Rhodochrosite in your bra (or simply holding one close to your heart) to maximize your attractiveness to those around you, and help you mesmerize everyone you meet. **Alternative gemstones:** Amber, Imperial Topaz, Sunstone.

Keeping your partner interested A Red Garnet in the bedroom will reignite your partner's passion for you and yours for them. Your relationship will turn from fizzling to sizzling before you know it. **Alternative gemstones:** Sardonyx, Emerald, Blue Sapphire.

Unrequited love Place a piece of Fuchsite by your heart to overcome the pain of unrequited love. The gem will soothe your sadness quicker than a box of your favorite chocolates, and help you remember what a catch you are. **Alternative gemstones:** Chrysocolla, Rhodonite, Lavender Jade.

Betrayal Feeling more bitter than an artichoke? Give your heart an emotional overhaul by placing a Dioptase crystal over a photo of your ex. Spend five minutes sending them kind thoughts each night, and you'll soon notice your anger lessen. **Alternative gemstones:** Amethyst, Agate, Pink Kunzite.

FEAR OF HEARTBREAK

Many people have real difficulty in allowing someone to get too close for fear of rejection and unbearable heartache. By not giving love a chance they miss so much that life has to offer. If you find yourself in this position, there are several things you can do.

First, banish any fears of rejection by holding a Cassiterite crystal to help you find the approval you seek within, and empower you to rely on yourself, rather than others, for acceptance. A Pink Petalite pushed into the soil of a potted plant can encourage you to share your love with another. Visualize it helping your heart to unfurl like the petals of your beautiful flowers. Then a Crystalline Kyanite held by your heart will help you to overcome your hang-ups and embrace your date with destiny. Remember that fortune favors the brave and no one deserves to be favored more than you. Make this your mantra by writing it down and putting it in a pouch with an Ajoite to lessen your fear of giving your heart to another person.

Alternative gemstones:
Cassiterite: Strawberry Quartz, Lavender Pink Smithsonite, Pink Sapphire.
Pink Petalite: Rhodochrosite, Pink Daburite, Manganoan Calcite.
Crystalline Kyanite: Green Tourmaline, Hemimorphite, Blue Lace Agate.
Ajoite: Blue Quartz, Flint, Eudialyte.

CASSITERITE

CRYSTALLINE KYANITE

AJOITE

CHRYSOCOLLA

DIOPTASE

CROCOITE

MELANITE

Divorce Ease the pain of your divorce by wearing a Crocoite necklace to help you remember the good times you shared together, and empower you to see the lessons, and blessings, in your heartbreak. **Alternative gemstones:** Melanite, Sulfur, Snowflake Obsidian.

Communication in relationships
Breathe new life into your relationship by placing a Green Tourmaline crystal in a potted plant, and leaving it beside a photo of you and your partner. The gem is said to encourage growth in everything—from romance and finances to shrubbery!—and will help your love blossom. **Alternative gemstones:** Kyanite, Aquamarine, Larimar.

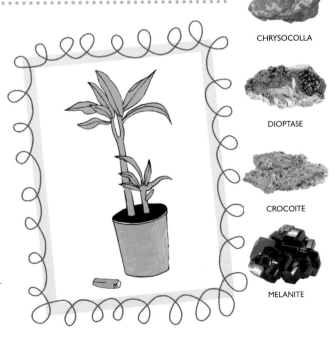

Empowerment Learn how to fall in love without being subsumed by holding a Pink Tourmaline by your heart to help you feel happy, contented, and whole—with or without someone at home. **Alternative gemstones:** Pink Halite, Rhodonite, Uvarovite Garnet.

Envy in relationships According to an old Cherokee legend, we each have two wolves inside us, one called fear, the other named love. The wolf that comes out on top is the one we feed most. Wear a Sugilite necklace to prevent fear from outgrowing, or destroying, love in your relationship. **Alternative gemstones:** Peridot, Rhodochrosite, Amethyst.

Express your emotions Hold a Blue Chalcedony by your throat to help you speak from your heart, and give you the courage to reveal your deepest thoughts and emotions, rather than keeping them hidden. **Alternative gemstones:** Blue Quartz, Cobaltoan Calcite, Azurite.

Sexual confidence Unleash your inner sex queen (or king!) by placing a piece of Pink Crackle Quartz by your bed to help you shed any inhibitions that may be holding you back, and ensure you are able to fully express your sexual needs. **Alternative gemstones:** Garnet, Turquoise, Opal.

Anxiety about love Open your heart to love as though it's never been broken by holding a Watermelon Tourmaline. The gem will prevent your previous heartaches from tainting your faith in fairytale romances, and ensure you never lose hope in your happy ending. **Alternative gemstones:** Celestite, Sunstone, Dioptase.

Previous partners Most of us want to keep the ones who've hurt us as far away as possible, yet often bring them closer than ever by locking them in our hearts. Hold a Tugtupite over your heart to help you forgive the pain your ex has caused you, but never forget the lessons the relationship taught you. **Alternative gemstones:** Stibnite, Rhodonite, Rainbow Obsidian.

THE POWER CRYSTAL: ROSE QUARTZ

Astrological signs: Taurus and Libra

Planet: Venus

Elements: Earth and Water

Chakra: Heart

Steeped in mystery and magic, **Rose Quartz** has a rich and fascinating history. It has been highly prized for its powerful healing properties from as far back as 600 BCE. Synonymous with unconditional love, joy, and healing, the beautiful pink crystal is thought to have been created by the Greek god Eros, who was so saddened by the suffering of others that he produced the gem to wash away the world's sorrow, and bring warmth and happiness into the hearts of its children. Like the calming scent of the beautiful flower the crystal is named after, a naturally reassuring energy emanates from the stone, encouraging us to feel completely safe and at peace with ourselves. **Rose Quartz** promotes sensitivity, empathy, and compassion for ourselves and others. It's believed to bring happiness, romance, and beauty to anyone who beholds it, and gently urges us to remember that we are worthy of love. If you've never received love, have recently lost someone special, or have been deeply wounded by the thorns of a past relationship, **Rose Quartz** will restore your faith in brighter days, and bring you the comfort, self-trust, and courage to open your heart again, knowing the love you seek, and so truly deserve, is on its way.

Gem-scriptions

Attracting love: Place a Rose Quartz crystal under your pillow to draw your perfect partner into your life, and keep you looking super-radiant and youthful.

Relationships: Display a few of the gems in each room to promote a loving, romantic atmosphere.

Self-love: Wear a Rose Quartz necklace to bathe your heart in self-loving energy, and help you accept yourself wholeheartedly.

love cocktails ... enhance your romantic life

Rose Quartz + **Chrysocolla** = stabilize a rocky relationship

Rose Quartz + **Chyrosprase** = overcome jealousy

Rose Quartz + **Imperial Topaz** = improve self-confidence and become more extroverted

THE POWER CRYSTAL: RUBY

Astrological signs: Leo, Cancer, Scorpio, Sagittarius

Planet: Mars

Element: Fire

Chakra: Heart

Fiery and captivating, **Ruby** is considered a truly regal gem. In ancient times, it was believed to be more valuable than all other precious stones and the Chinese Emperor Kublai Khan (1215–1294) is believed to have offered an entire city in exchange for a large **Ruby**.

In the ancient Sanskrit language, this crystal is known as 'ratnaraj,' which translates as 'King of Gemstones' and the stone has been revered in many cultures throughout history. This stunning red stone represents devotion, desire, and passion, and is a symbol of eternal love.

The **Ruby** is also associated with prediction and, in the Middle Ages, it was considered to be a stone of prophecy that would darken when its wearer was in danger. In the 16th and 17th centuries, curative properties were also attributed to the stone and it was thought to counteract poison.

Wearing a striking piece of **Ruby** jewelry will bring good health, wisdom, and luck in love. It is a gem for true romantics and will help to fan the flames of desire in your relationship.

Gem-scriptions

Spice up Your Relationship: Wear a Ruby ring to increase the passion in your relationship and keep the flame of love alive.

Insightfulness: If you're unsure whether or not to purse a new relationship, hold a Ruby while thinking about the new person in your life. The gem will enhance your intuition and you'll soon know if you've met Mr. (or Ms.) Right.

Moving On: When you are struggling to get over a failed relationship, wear a Ruby over your heart to bring you healing and comfort, and attract new passions into your life.

love cocktails ... enhance your romantic life

Ruby + Morganite = improve your sex life

Ruby + Fuchsite = provides clarity if you are faced with a confusing love dilemma

Ruby + Zoisite = dissolve the painful feelings of unrequited love

Freedom in relationships

Make sure being love-struck doesn't leave you feeling trapped by creating an "I'm fabulous" box and filling it with memories of fun times you've had without your partner. Look through it each night with a Lepidolite by your heart to ensure that "me" doesn't become "we." **Alternative gemstones:** Rhodonite, Sunstone, Blue-Green Smithsonite.

PERIDOT

Guilt in relationships

All actions come from one of two places—love or fear. A relationship consumed by the latter is likely to lead to stress. Banish any distrust between you and your partner by keeping a Lavender-Pink Smithsonite in your bedroom. **Alternative gemstones:** Rose Quartz, Peridot, Larimar.

CELESTITE

Take a new relationship forward

Turn Mr or Mrs Possible into marriage material by wearing a Chrysanthemum Stone necklace on your next date, holding one close to your heart, or slipping one into your bra, to keep the attraction and passion between you sky high. **Alternative gemstones:** Ametrine, Merlinite, Celestite.

BERYL

Reinvigorate stale relationships

Reignite the passion between you and your partner so it flares like a candle brightening up a dark room. Treat them to a candlelit meal, give Beryl as a gift, and keep one under your pillow to rekindle the flame between you. **Alternative gemstones:** Morganite, Emerald, Diamond.

ELBAITE

Harmony in love

Stay serene when your partner forgets to run errands or do chores by writing a list of everything you love about them, and reading through it with a Green Jade by your heart to prevent any little quirks from driving you crazy. It will keep the peace between you. **Alternative gemstones:** Emerald, Rose Quartz, Fluorite.

Healing a broken heart

Hold an Elbaite over your heart, and imagine it putting the pieces back together, just like a beautiful stained-glass window, and creating an even more magnificent whole from the broken fragments. **Alternative gemstones:** Eudialyte, Chrysocolla, Rose Elestial Quartz.

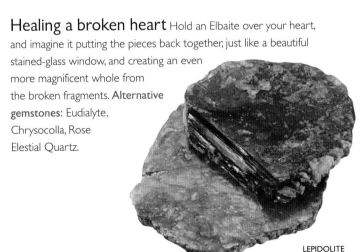

LEPIDOLITE

Crystal Fact

Emeralds don't just fire up your relationships, but your libido too. They are an excellent aphrodisiac.

Painful memories

Reflecting on the past can bring such sweet sadness. We long for the times we were happiest, and rue the ones we were saddest. Hold a Cacoxenite by your heart to help you see the positive, however small, in your melancholy memories. **Alternative gemstones:** Stibnite, Strawberry Quartz, Goethite.

The art of seduction

Embrace your inner sex kitten by placing a Ruby under your mattress to maximize your sexual confidence, and ensure you master the art of seduction to purr-fection! **Alternative gemstones:** Thulite, Garnet, Quantum Quattro.

Individuality in relationships

If you have a soul—which I'm assuming you do, unless you're a vampire!—and are your own mate, guess what? You've already got a soul mate! Hold a Chinese Chromium Quartz to remind you of that, and ensure you turn the "w" in "we" upside down, and focus on "me" from time to time. **Alternative gemstones:** Pyrophyllite, Quantum Quattro, Candle Quartz.

Feeling tied down

The next time you start feeling overwhelmed, write an essential must-do list, and wear a Vera Cruz Amethyst necklace to help you clarify what's necessary (cooking your partner dinner) and what's over-generous (giving said partner a foot rub), and ensure you say "hell no" to the latter. **Alternative gemstones:** Shift Crystal Quartz, Tanzanite, Chrysoberyl.

Spice up your relationship

Swap mild and nice for hot and spicy by wearing a Falcon's Eye necklace to help you shed your inhibitions in bed, and ensure your clothes aren't the only things you throw off when the lights go off, but your insecurities, too. **Alternative gemstones:** Gray-Banded Agate, Covellite, Quantum Quattro.

CHALCEDONY

GOETHITE

THULITE

CHRYSOBERYL

COVELLITE

ANGEL AURA QUARTZ

Keep your spirits up When you're head over heels, but the object of your affections is playing it cool and hasn't called, play a defiant anthem and have yourself a singsong. Hold a Silver Leaf Jasper in one hand, a hairbrush in the other, and mime along in a mirror to feel better in no time. **Alternative gemstones:** Angel Aura Quartz, Chalcedony, Pink-Banded Agate.

Chasing away singleton blues Chasing love is a bit like trying to catch a butterfly—the more you grasp at it, the farther away it flies. Wear an Abalone Shell to help you feel less lonely without a partner, and inspire you to stop chasing butterflies and wait for the one who gives them to you. **Alternative gemstones:** Manganoan Calcite, Watermelon Tourmaline, Rose Quartz.

ABALONE SHELL

LOOKING FOR LOVE

First you have to learn to love yourself. Otherwise, looking for love is like going shopping without a purse—pointless, painful, and guaranteed to end in tears. When you feel ready for a new relationship, give your heart an emotional detox by holding a piece of Chrysocolla to help you draw a line under previous disappointments, and wearing a Shift Quartz to ensure your most valuable accessory—self-love—is in abundant supply.

Then create a vision board and fill it with images of your ideal mate. Be specific and include all the lovely things you would like to do together. Look at it each night with a Roselite by your heart. You could also give Cupid a nudge by writing a list of all the things you're looking for in a partner, and reading it each night with a Blue Aragonite by your heart to help you visualize someone sweeping you off your feet. A quieter way to discover your romantic fate is to spend five minutes holding a Rose Quartz just before you go to bed, and asking it to show you, while you sleep, who you're destined to meet. Then, your ritual of choice performed, snuggle down, knowing that sweet dreams of your future lover await you.

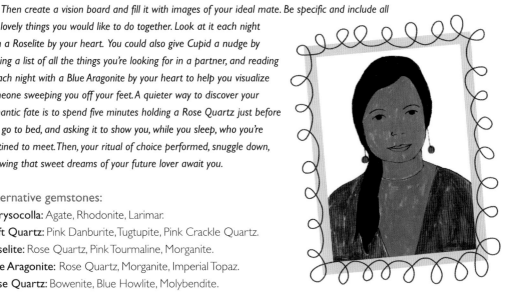

Alternative gemstones:
Chrysocolla: Agate, Rhodonite, Larimar.
Shift Quartz: Pink Danburite, Tugtupite, Pink Crackle Quartz.
Roselite: Rose Quartz, Pink Tourmaline, Morganite.
Blue Aragonite: Rose Quartz, Morganite, Imperial Topaz.
Rose Quartz: Bowenite, Blue Howlite, Molybendite.

Moving forward

Swap past unhappiness for brighter tomorrows by writing a list of everything you'd like to release, and burning it with a candle flame. Bury the ashes in your garden, along with a Charoite crystal and some seeds, and both you and your plant will soon flourish. **Alternative gemstones:** Gypsum, Chevron Amethyst, Dalmatian Stone.

First-date confidence

Ease into your first date by adding a pair of Zircon earrings to your outfit (or keeping one in your pocket) to enhance your personal magnetism, and ensure the only thing running away from you is the time! **Alternative gemstones:** Hematite, Imperial Topaz, Boulder Opal.

Don't be hung-up on past loves

They say every relationship teaches you something, so technically the more you have, the wiser you become! Affirm this to yourself any time you start missing an old lover, and hold a Green Obsidian to help you remember that sometimes new beginnings can only come from unhappy endings. **Alternative gemstones:** Halite, Pink Petalite, Yellow Smithsonite.

Being spontaneous

In a world where mere chance can lead to wedding bells, you never know what's going to happen. You could walk out of your house, trip, fall, and land yourself a spouse! Hold a Rutilated Topaz to attract love into your life. **Alternative gemstones:** Rose Quartz, Rhodochrosite, Pink Tourmaline.

HALITE

Nurturing love

Roses are synonymous with romance. Treat yourself to a rose bush and pop an Erythrite in the soil to encourage the love between you and your new partner to flower—like your lovely roses—and fill your life with beauty. **Alternative gemstones:** Green Tourmaline, Yttrian Fluorite, Emerald.

ERYTHRITE

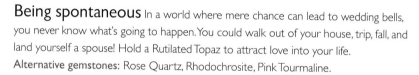

GREEN TOURMALINE

Rekindling love

Reawaken the love between you and your partner by taking a fragranced bath together. Light a rose-scented candle and have some romantic music playing softly. A Lithium Quartz on the side will make all the difference. **Alternative gemstones:** Vivianite, Beryl, Aegirine.

VIVIANITE

Getting over the one who got away

We all have someone who we can't quite seem to shake from our minds—a first love perhaps, or an ex-partner. Write that person a love letter while holding an Orchid Calcite, put it in an envelope with a few rose petals, and throw it into a lake or river to wash away your heart's ache. **Alternative gemstones:** Pink Petalite, Manganoan Calcite, Rainbow Obsidian.

Staying faithful

In ancient times, people would keep Emeralds in their homes to encourage faithfulness in relationships. Place one in your bedroom to keep the flame of love between you and your partner burning brightly. **Alternative gemstones:** Blue Tourmaline, Diamond, Chrysoprase.

Going through a rough patch

A couple who had been married for 65 years were asked the secret to their long and happy relationship. They replied that they were from a time when you fixed something that was broken, rather than just throwing it away. Hold a Black Moonstone to ensure you and your partner do the same, and find the strength to work through the difficult patches that all couples go through. **Alternative gemstones:** Beryl, Larimar, Manganoan Calcite.

Unconditional love

"Even after all this time, the sun never says to the Earth, 'you owe me.' Look what happens with a love like that, it lights the whole sky." The poet Hafiz beautifully described unconditional love in these lines. Place a Chrysoberyl somewhere visible to keep the love between you and your partner invincible. **Alternative gemstones:** Rose Quartz, Pink Danburite, Petalite.

Forgiveness

Betrayal is the drop of ink that taints love's canvas; forgiveness is the water you throw on it to weaken its power. Hold a Khutnohorite to help you forgive your partner's mistakes. **Alternative gemstones:** Rhodonite, Rhodochrosite, Chrysoberyl.

Opening your heart to love

When we have been burned by the fire of love, many of us allow our hearts to become cold. We refuse to believe that we can love again after a failed affair. Freeze a few rose petals, hold a Yellow Crackle Quartz, and watch the petals melt to prevent your heart from staying frozen. **Alternative gemstones:** Roselite, Pink Tourmaline, Eudialyte.

MANGANOAN CALCITE

RAINBOW OBSIDIAN

DIAMOND

BLACK MOONSTONE

LARIMAR

PETALITE

RHODONITE

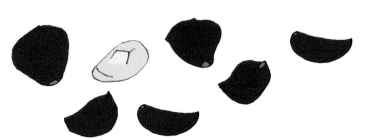

Bonding with your partner
Marriage isn't about falling in love with one person once, but falling in love with the same person every day. Keep an Ametrine in your bedroom to prevent the spark between you from fading away, and ensure you fall more in love with each other each day. **Alternative gemstones:** Celestite, Chrysanthemum Stone, Celestite.

Don't be influenced by negativity from others
Our dating choices are just that—ours. Sometimes your friends might be surprised at your choice of partner. They might have your best interests at heart, but they could also be motivated by their own negativity or jealousy. Hold a Schorl to prevent other people's negativity from affecting your love life. **Alternative gemstones:** Amber, Cassiterite, Diamond.

AMETRINE

Don't be a cynic
It's never too late to meet your perfect mate. Affirm this to yourself by hanging a heart pendant on a chain (with a Marble) any time you start feeling sceptical. This will remind you that it's very often when we're at our most cynical that love turns around and hands us a miracle. **Alternative gemstones:** Merlinite, Chrysoberyl, Iceland Spar.

Toxic exes
Ex becoming a pest? Don't stress—hold a Pyrolusite by your chest! The gem's an absolute must for dealing with exes, and will prevent you from wasting time on Mr or Ms Wrong. **Alternative gemstones:** Eudialyte, Amblygonite, Stibnite.

PYROLUSITE

Meeting the in-laws
Worried your in-laws will think you're a bore? Don't fret, simply add a Chalcedony to your evening ensemble to ensure they're super-impressed with your charisma and charm. **Alternative gemstones:** Chrysoberyl, Spinel, Alexandrite.

WATERMELON TOURMALINE

Crystal Fact
The name "Diamond" comes from the Greek word "adamas," meaning "invincible."

Wedding-day nerves
Prevent nerves from spoiling your special day by rubbing a piece of Dalmatian Stone any time you start feeling stressed to keep any negative emotions in check. **Alternative gemstones:** Watermelon Tourmaline, Abalone Shell, Amazonite.

BREAKING UP

Everything ends. Endings are a part of life just as much as beginnings, and inevitably we have to learn to cope with them. Sometimes we don't know how strong we are until we're thrown into the ocean without a float, and realize we knew how to swim all along. Sometimes we have to fall apart, like beautiful but slightly cracked china, not because we're too weak to hold ourselves together, but because we're strong enough to know we can be better, and we deserve better.

A Xenotime will help you to remember how well you were doing before your lost love affair, and to understand that you will love again, and a Peach Selenite will ensure you carry on to become the best version of yourself you can be. An Amblygonite hung on a chain with a butterfly pendant will remind you that your heart's broken wings will soon mend.

As a form of therapy, start a "wisdom journal." Jot down anything you could have done differently, while holding a Hawk's Eye, to help you accept responsibility for your part in the relationship's breakdown. Then wash away any lingering sadness with an Apache Tear and use it to help you rise from the ashes of heartache like a phoenix, feeling stronger, braver, and more emotionally liberated than ever.

Alternative gemstones:
Xenotine: Charoite, Cobaltoan Calcite, Moss Agate.
Peach Selenite: Unakite, Muscovite, Ethiopian Opal.
Amblygonite: Moonstone, Peridot, Smoky Quartz.
Hawk's Eye: Rhodonite, Rhodochrosite, Snow Quartz.
Apache Tear: Manganoan Calcite, Obsidian, Pink Sapphire.

DALMATIAN STONE

Arguments
Disagreements are like a game of chess—they need two people to play. Walk away from them and no one can win. Wear an Afghanite ring on one of your fingers to prevent you from picking petty fights. **Alternative gemstones:** Tugtupite, Limonite, Sugilite.

SUGILITE

Finding love in your later years
"Nothing in nature is hurried, yet everything is accomplished." Lao Tzu's maxim also applies to true love. You can't judge a seed before it's been sown, or hurry a flower to bloom. Hold a Green Aventurine to help you patiently await love's arrival. **Alternative gemstones:** Morganite, Pink Tourmaline, Rose Quartz.

APACHE TEAR

Working through problems
Relationships—like a story—are a work in progress. They're never finished, not really. They can always be rewritten, revised, and edited. Hold a Quantum Quattro to prevent the glitches in one chapter from making you write off your happy ever after. **Alternative gemstones:** Eudialyte, Erythrite, Rose Quartz.

MERLINITE

Find a last-minute date
Looking for a date as your plus one for a special event? Simply wear a Morganite around your neck for a few days before the big event, and you can be sure you won't be turning up alone! **Alternative gemstones:** Rose Quartz, Morganite, Blue Aragonite.

Resentment in relationships
People used to believe Topaz crystals produced their own light, and mariners would often use the gems to guide them when it was dark. Wear one to guide you and your partner through your sadness and help you find the light of your love when things feel dark. **Alternative gemstones:** Faden Quartz, Beryl, Opal.

Enduring love
When it comes to love, you can't beat a dove! The birds are believed to mate for life, staying with the same partner forever. Place an image of a pair of turtledoves in your home, alongside a Lapis Lazuli, to inspire you and your partner to mate for life, too. **Alternative gemstones:** Green Sapphire, Diamond, Tugtupite.

Sexual insecurity
Sex and love are like strawberries and cream—fabulous alone, but even better together. Fear and insecurity are like tweezing and waxing—awful alone, and even worse together! Wear a Smoky Quartz to ensure you feed strawberries and cream to the partner of your dreams. **Alternative gemstones:** Turquoise, Pink Crackle Quartz, Garnet.

Sexual connection
According to Chinese legend, Yue Lao, a deity who sits under the moon, ties an invisible red string between those who are destined to marry. Hang a Crystalline Kyanite on a red thread to help you and your partner feel more connected. **Alternative gemstones:** Erythrite, African Jade, Rose Quartz.

Sexual droughts
The crystal Rutilated Quartz is often referred to as Venus's Hair Stone, because it's thought to contain pieces of the love goddess's hair. Wear one around your neck the next time you and your partner go through a dry spell to help you get the chemistry back. **Alternative gemstones:** Variscite, Beryl, Lapis Lazuli.

Crystal Fact

Lapis Lazuli is thought to boost your chances of becoming famous.

Sexual passion Swap sexual frustration for hot loving action by keeping a Red Jasper in your bedroom to help you shine like a star, and ensure things stay passionate between the sheets.
Alternative gemstones: Red Garnet, Red-Black Obsidian, Poppy Jasper.

Toxic partners Some relationships are like mirrors—they help us to see ourselves in all our glory, but they are also fragile and easily broken. Hold a Rainbow Obsidian to prevent you from cutting yourself by trying to piece together something that can't be fixed. **Alternative gemstones:** Obsidian, Aventurine, Peridot.

Crystal Fact

The name "Aventurine" comes from the Italian term "a ventura," meaning "by chance."

Predicting the future

Love life a bore? Find out what's in store by popping a few gems in a pouch and asking for guidance. Then pick one randomly and trust its meaning.

Moss Agate: love could blossom with someone you know.
Emerald: romance with an ex.
Moonstone: a new relationship.
Blue Lace Agate: reveal your feelings to someone on whom you have a crush.
Chrysotile: let go of your ex.
Ruby: a passionate love affair.

RUTILATED QUARTZ

RED JASPER

MOSS AGATE

EMERALD

BLUE LACE AGATE

Know that you are already whole

Relationships aren't about finding someone to complete you; if you've got a mind, body, and soul, you're already whole. Wear a Lepidolite to help you overcome your timidity on dates, and realize that a soul mate's a mate for the soul, not someone to make it whole. **Alternative gemstones:** Rhodonite, Iolite, Vera Cruz Amethyst.

OBSIDIAN

Trust in relationships

The ancient Greeks and Romans believed Cupid's arrows were dipped in Diamonds before he fired them, giving them a power unlike any other. Wear one around your neck to ensure you believe in the arrows you catch. **Alternative gemstones:** Pink Agate, Rhodochrosite, Larimar.

PERIDOT

LEPIDOLITE

RHODONITE

Up the X (rated)-factor

Inject some fiery passion into your bedtime action by picking a gem to keep things superhot. Make it fun by keeping a bag of gems by your bed and taking it in turns to choose your treat for the night! Here are a few ideas:

Rhodochrosite: play a sexy tune.
Aquamarine: make love in the tub.
Dendritic Quartz: get x-rated outdoors.
Rose Quartz: read each other poetry.
Turquoise: talk dirty.
Opal: share your fantasies.

RHODOCHROSITE

Rebuilding trust

In 1750 a clever Parisian jeweller created Pink Topaz crystals when he discovered that the yellow variety turned pink when exposed to heat. Hold the gem by your heart to help you to forgive a partner's dishonesty. **Alternative gemstones:** Diopside, Graphic Smoky Quartz, Pink Tourmaline.

Be an army of two

A French fairytale, La Chatte Blanche (The White Cat), tells the story of a prince who falls in love with a princess. But the princess has been turned into a cat by evil fairies. He breaks the spell by kissing her and they return to his father's castle wearing Rubies. Wear one to help you and your prince or princess unite against evil. **Alternative gemstones:** Diamond, Sardonyx, Green Sapphire.

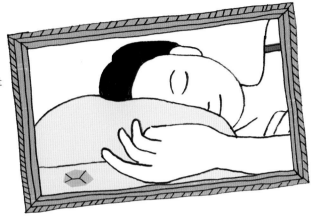

Renewing love

According to Inuit legend, there was once a reindeer girl called Tutu, who fled to the mountains to give birth to her first child. Her life-producing blood seeped into the stones, creating what we now call Tugtupite gemstones. Wear one to help you renew your love with your partner. **Alternative gemstones:** Beryl, Rose Quartz, Crystalline Kyanite.

A zest for romance

According to legend, St Valentine (widely considered to be the patron saint of lovers) wore an Amethyst ring with an image of Cupid engraved on it. Wear one to inspire you to believe in love, just like he did. **Alternative gemstones:** Cobaltoan Calcite, Pink Topaz, Pink Tourmaline.

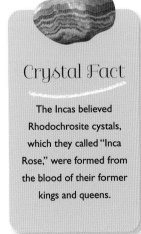

Crystal Fact

The Incas believed Rhodochrosite cystals, which they called "Inca Rose," were formed from the blood of their former kings and queens.

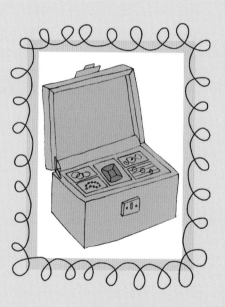

Chapter 2
Home & Family

Crystals for Home & Family

SMOKY ROSE QUARTZ

ONYX

AGATE

Families can be a bit like chocolate—wonderful in small quantities, but not so good if you have too much. But, as any chocolate-lover will tell you, the sweeter moments are definitely worth the sicklier ones. So in this chapter, I'm going to look at ways of helping you appreciate the delights in your family chocolate box, and empower you to say no—and stick to it—when you've had enough, and need some "me time."

Using **Red Phantom Quartz**, I'll work on healing the scars of any toxic sweets, such as anger, resentment, or guilt, your parents fed you as a child, and ensuring the ones you feed your own children are filled with affection, sprinkled with acceptance, and served with a big mug of love. This remarkable crystal will help you to feel grounded and able to look at yourself at a deeper level. This introspection will allow you to heal your inner child, break old, unhelpful patterns, and recover repressed memories.

Of course, happy families need happy homes, so I'll look at ways of keeping your home welcoming and loving, using **Smoky Rose Quartz**, **Brown Tourmaline**, and **Spirit Quartz**. The best gems for helping you cope when your children misbehave, suffer from nightmares, and eventually leave home are featured, too, as are tips on dealing with teenage temper tantrums and naughty pets. **Spirit Quartz** is particularly helpful when your family structure is going through a period of change. It facilitates bonding in the home, especially when a new member joins the family, perhaps a new baby or an adopted child.

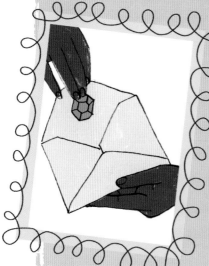

Advice on the best gems for silencing noisy neighbors is included, along with suggestions for protecting your home from negative energy, neighborhood busybodies, and meddling relatives, using **Onyx**, **Agate**, and **Rutilated Quartz**. **Agate** is believed to help you discern the truth, so it's a perfect gem to use when you're dealing with a family conflict where all sides are blaming one another! This crystal is also a powerful emotional healer and so, as well as helping you to understand the roots of a family argument, it will also help you to heal the rift.

There's even advice on the top gems for helping your plants grow, and keeping your fruit and vegetables fresh! So whether you're seeking to heal a childhood wound, or want to help your own children bloom, this chapter will help you ensure your home is always full of happiness and laughter.

RUTILATED QUARTZ

BROWN TOURMALINE

SPIRIT QUARTZ

Heal rifts, strengthen bonds, and ensure your home is filled with happiness...

Your Crystal Tips for Home & Family

ROSE QUARTZ

MOONSTONE

CITRINE

CHRYSOCOLLA

BOWENITE

GREEN FLUORITE

OBSIDIAN

Communication at home
Put a Spirit Quartz gemstone beside a photo of your family to spread a kind and loving energy through your abode, like a candle scenting the air, and to ensure everyone gets along. **Alternative gemstones:** Jade, Rose Quartz, Moonstone.

Harmony at home
Even the most saintly person gets annoyed sometimes. Place a Brown Tourmaline in your living room to avoid arguments with loved ones, and create a harmonious atmosphere. **Alternative gemstones:** Spirit Quartz, Citrine, Chrysocolla.

CRYSTALS AND MOVING HOUSE

Selling your home is always a stressful business, but you can make it less so by placing a Purpurite crystal in each of your rooms, and a large one in the hallway. This creates an inviting vibe, which will attract plenty of prospective buyers.

Once you have moved, whether to a new area, a new country, or just down the road, your new home marks a fresh start. A Bowenite crystal by your new front door will dissolve any attachments to the past, and a Cerussite will inspire you to walk through it completely baggage-free (emotionally that is, not literally!)

Crystal Fact

Forget concealer! Jade is the ultimate spot-buster, and will blitz your zits in no time!

Alternative gemstones:
Purpurite: Novaculite, Citrine, Pyrite.
Bowenite: Green Fluorite, Obsidian, Citrine.
Cerussite: Meteorite, Bowenite, Brown Jade.

THE POWER CRYSTAL: EMERALD

Astrological sign: Aries, Taurus, Gemini

Planet: Venus

Element: Earth

Chakra: Heart

Emeralds have captivated the hearts and minds of people from all over the world from as far back as 4,000 BCE, and were once thought to contain the very essence of nature in their mesmerizing splendor. Known as "the stone of domestic bliss," the gem encourages us to remain rooted like a tree, to flower like a plant, and to give and receive nurture like everything in nature.

Encouraging us to declare our love as if we'll die tomorrow, and share it as though we'll live forever, these beautiful stones inspire us to love without condition, observe without judgment, and unite with those we cherish. Indeed, some of the world's greatest love stories began with an **Emerald**, from the stunning engagement ring Prince Rainier gave Grace Kelly when he proposed—turning her from an actress into a princess—to the **Emerald** earrings, bracelet, and necklace Richard Burton gave his own princess, Elizabeth Taylor, as an engagement gift. If our relationships with our loved ones are the roses in our souls' gardens, **Emeralds** are the gardeners who water their soil.

So whether you're seeking to sow seeds of forgiveness, water the "roses" in your family garden, or simply marvel at the beautiful flowers around you, this gem is the one to turn to.

Gem-scriptions

Healing rifts: Mend a broken relationship by writing a list of things you miss about your loved one, and sending it to them with an Emerald and photo of the two of you together to renew the bond between you.

Deepening: Pop an Emerald, which is associated with growth, in a plant pot, and place it beside a family photograph to help nurture the love between you.

Appreciation: Wear an Emerald necklace to ensure you tell those closest to you how much you love them.

family cocktails ... supercharge the gem's power

Emerald + Pink Crackle Quartz = heal childhood wounds

Emerald + Pink Agate = deepen bond between parents and children

Emerald + Spirit Quartz = avoid petty arguments with loved ones

Emerald + Stibnite = prevent loved ones from snooping through your emails!

CRYSTALS AND NEIGHBORS

In a busy world of work, family, and existing friends, it can be easy to forget that new friendship opportunities may present themselves right on your doorstep. Place a Stone of Solidarity by your door to inspire you to spread your social net, and when spending time with a neighbor, hold a Chrysopal. This will ensure you don't overlook the gems in your neighborhood's treasure chest. Some people are like the crystals in this book—so small from afar, but more enchanting and powerful up close.

Of course, neighbors are not always a blessing. Some can be noisy, overly inquisitive, or downright unpleasant. The next time your new, music-loving neighbors start playing their favorite songs loudly, forget throwing a hissy fit. Simply hold a Pyrite to prevent you from taking life so seriously, and ensure they soon stop their raucousness. And when Mildred from next door starts poking about your business, give her the brush-off gem-style by placing a few Agate crystals by your front entrance. This will stop nosy neighbors from prying into your affairs.

They say revenge is a dish best served cold. Fiddlesticks! It's a dish guaranteed to leave you lying awake at night with "mood" poisoning until it's out of your system! Hold a Fluorapatite to help you overcome any hostility toward your neighbors. In general, though, neighborhood drama is best avoided and you can protect your home's karma by placing a Cervanite by your front door. This will prevent other people's wars from affecting you and yours, and ensure neighborhood gripes don't keep you up at night.

Crystal Fact

Pyrite not only helps you sell your home, but is also an absolute must for silencing noisy neighbors.

Alternative gems

Stone of Solidarity: Barite, Turquoise, Bowenite.
Chrysopal: Blue Quartz, Flint, Sardonyx.
Pyrite: Watermelon Tourmaline, Geothite, Pyromorphite.
Agate: Hematite, Selenite, Obsidian.
Fluorapatite: Ametrine, Aquamarine, Sugilite.
Cervanite: Bloodstone, Agate, Amethyst.

Bring gratitude into your home

"There are always flowers for those who want to see them"—artist Henri Matisse. Heed his advice by treating yourself to a bouquet of your favorite blooms each week, and placing an Eilat Stone by them to inspire you to see the roses rather than the thorns in every garden. **Alternative gemstones:** Pietersite, Cavansite, Nebula Stone.

Tired parents

Stop being a pushover, and fix your kids' bad behavior by taking a deep breath, closing your eyes, and rubbing a Tiger Iron to help you cope with their naughty antics, and prevent them from making you lose your temper. **Alternative gemstones:** Mookaite, Pink Agate, Chrysoberyl.

New mom

Surf through your first birth by keeping a Pink Agate crystal by your heart to encourage your maternal instincts to kick in, and a bond to develop between you and your bundle of joy. **Alternative gemstones:** Chalcedony, Rose Quartz, Mookaite.

Stop your little ones from having bad dreams

Protect your children from nightly frights by slipping a Pentagonite under their pillows, or leave one by their window, to prevent bad dreams from keeping them awake. **Alternative gemstones:** Ruby, Celestite, Flint.

Crystal Fact

Tiger Iron is thought to enhance your artistic talents.

Feeling broody

Prevent your desire to become a parent from smothering the love that already exists between you and your partner by holding a Red-Brown Agate by your heart. This will help to remind you that patience is a virtue and good things come to those who wait. **Alternative gemstones:** Blood of Isis, Zincite, Hematoid Calcite.

Overcoming your parenting mistakes

All parents make mistakes—even Buddha's father kept him locked away for years to protect him from the world's suffering, potentially denying us a whole faith—so, in the grander scheme of things, you're doing OK. Hold a Tangerine Quartz to ensure you know that. **Alternative gemstones:** Snowflake Obsidian, Chrysoprase, Rose Quartz.

BLUE QUARTZ

THE POWER CRYSTAL: ONYX

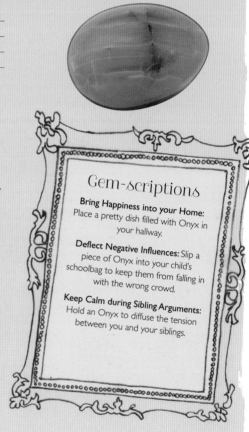

Astrological sign: Leo
Planets: Mars and Saturn
Element: Earth
Chakra: Base

Although the dark and mysterious black **Onyx** is very well-known, the **Onyx** is actually a type of chalcedony and comes in a variety of colours.

In Roman mythology, the **Onyx** is truly a stone of the goddess. Legend has it that Venus, the goddess of love and beauty, was one day resting on the banks of a river. As she rested, Cupid used the point of one of his arrows to give her a manicure fit for a goddess! As no part of a goddess can ever really die, the clippings were metamorphosed into **Onyx** when they fell into the river. The word comes from the Greek onux, which means 'fingernail.'

This grounding stone will promote happiness and stability at home and peaceful familial relations. **Onyx** is a wonderful stone to use if you need to let go of past hurts such as sibling rivalry or a difficult relationship with your parents.

The stone also has powerful protective qualities and is often used as a defense against negativity from other people.

Onyx is also synonymous with self-mastery, inner strength, and resistance. It is a great gem to wear or carry when you need to bite your tongue or avoid lashing out at someone!

Gem-scriptions

Bring Happiness into your Home: Place a pretty dish filled with Onyx in your hallway.

Deflect Negative Influences: Slip a piece of Onyx into your child's schoolbag to keep them from falling in with the wrong crowd.

Keep Calm during Sibling Arguments: Hold an Onyx to diffuse the tension between you and your siblings.

home cocktails ... for harmonious relations

Onyx + Tiger Eye = stay grounded during stressful times

Onyx + Agate = create strong family bonds

Onyx + Iolite = protect your family from negative influences

Arguments

Arguments All families are slightly kooky, and those that aren't are even kookier for not being kooky. Learn to accept your relatives and place a Blue Agate in your living room to avoid silly squabbles with loved ones. **Alternative gemstones:** Diopside, Siberian Green Quartz, Green Agate.

Anger at home Stay Zen when your family's driving you around the bend by placing a Blue Moonstone in your living room to improve relations between you, and prevent you from throwing a temper tantrum (or an apple pie!) at anyone. **Alternative gemstones:** Spirit Quartz, Emerald, Agate.

Difficult teens Turn your troublesome teens into every parent's dream by slipping an Atlantasite under their mattresses to prevent any door-slamming temper tantrums, and help them become delightful people. **Alternative gemstones:** Stichtite, Stromatolite, Gray-Banded Agate.

BLUE AGATE

GREEN AGATE

NATURAL_QUARTZ

STICHTITE

BLUE MOONSTONE

CAVANSITE

GRAY-BANDED AGATE

CLEANSING YOUR HOME

A house full of negative energy can have an adverse effect on you and your family. Spritz each room with water in which a Clear Quartz has been left to soak in the sun for two hours to banish any harmful chi. You could also hang some pretty Natural Quartz crystals around your rooms, and dangle a few from banisters and window frames to liven up the atmosphere.

A Sulfur outside your front door will protect you all from negativity. The gem will watch over your home, like a powerful sphinx, and placing an Amethyst indoors will perform the same function. Amethysts are said to have been created when the goddess Diana turned a young maiden, Amethystos, into the gemstone to protect her from the unwanted attentions of the god Dionysus. So Amethysts are great for all forms of protection.

Alternative gems:
Clear Quartz: Smoky Rose Quartz, Malachite, Cavansite.
Natural Quartz: Moonstone, Onyx, Malachite.
Sulfur: Carnelian, Amethyst, Calcite.
Amethyst: Fire Opal, Cobalto Calcite, Uvite Tourmaline on Magnesite.

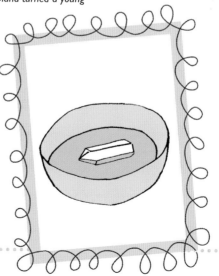

Meddling family

Prevent your nosy family from driving you crazy by placing a Rutilated Quartz in a potted plant, and leaving it outside your front door to protect you from their meddling tomfoolery, and stop them from interfering in your life choices. **Alternative gemstones:** Mookaite, Agate, Lavender Jade.

Say no to demanding relatives

Hold a Brazilianite crystal near your throat chakra to prevent you from caving in to others, despite any need to please. It will empower you to say no and stick to it the next time your sister-in-law asks for help with the garden pruning, for example. **Alternative gemstones:** Dumortierite, Blue Opal, Barite.

Build deeper bonds

Place a Datolite crystal beside a photo of you and your loved ones and keep it in your living room to remind you of the happy times you've shared together, and help you see the best in each other. **Alternative gemstones:** Emerald, Rose Quartz, Jade.

Freedom from overbearing parents

Stop your clingy mom and dad from driving you mad by sneaking a Botswana Agate under a photo of yourself in their home to encourage them to let you spread your wings and fly, knowing you'll return to their nest again soon. **Alternative gemstones:** Yellow Labradorite, Green Tourmaline, Nuummite.

Gratitude for loved ones

Life can break our hearts, but the love we have for our family and friends reminds us how lucky we are. Fill a box with memories of times you've shared, and look at it while holding a Green Sapphire by your heart to ensure you treasure the gems in your family jewelry box. **Alternative gemstones:** Ocean Jasper, Rose Quartz, Morganite.

RUTILATED QUARTZ

BRAZILIANITE

OCEAN JASPER

TOURMALINATED QUARTZ

CHILDHOOD SCARS

Many of us feel imprisoned by our pasts, not realizing we ourselves hold the keys to our freedom. Repair the childhood crosses you bear by holding a Sodalite by your heart. Picture yourself unlocking the door to your cage and setting yourself free, forgiving whoever you have been blaming. Forgiveness and anger are like fire and water—they cancel each other out. You can't be angry with someone if you've forgiven them, and you can't forgive someone if you're angry with them. Hold a Smithsonite to help you pour water on the fires that were lit when you were a kid.

If old hurts still prevent you from blooming, hang a Red Phantom Quartz on a locket that contains a photo of yourself as a child, and spend five minutes sending your younger self love and healing each evening. Any emotional scars left by your earlier life can be treated by holding a Fairy Quartz, and imagining it sewing your heart back together, like a beautiful tapestry, turning the leftover scraps of your childhood into a masterpiece.

What our parents say to us as children often becomes what we say to ourselves as adults. If their comments were good, that's great; if they were bad, it can lead to self-hate. So if that is the root of the problem, hold a Pineapple Amethyst to free yourself from critical parental comments.

Alternative gems

Sodalite: Dioptase, Smithsonite, Chrysoprase.
Smithsonite: Youngite, Diopside, Yellow Crackle Quartz.
Red Phantom Quartz: Kunzite, Muscovite, Chrysoprase.
Fairy Quartz: Malachite, Chrysoprase, Diopside.
Pineapple Amethyst: Red Phantom Quartz, Fairy Quartz, Quantum Quattro.

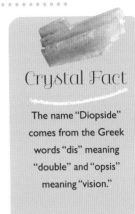

Crystal Fact

The name "Diopside" comes from the Greek words "dis" meaning "double" and "opsis" meaning "vision."

Crystal Fact

Sodalite is said to give you thicker skin.

SMITHSONITE

CRYSTALS AND ABSENCE

Parents give their children wings to fly, and inspire them to climb high and achieve their dreams, but sometimes it's difficult to let them go. Blood of Isis is a brilliant crystal to use for this. Hang one on a locket containing their picture, and hold it by your heart any time it aches for them; and place a Cat's Eye Quartz beside another photograph to ensure you never stop seeing the hero in them.

The absence of any loved ones can be hard to bear. There was once an Earth goddess named Demeter whose daughter, Persephone, was abducted by Hades and taken to the Underworld, where she was forced to spend half the year. Demeter mourned this time without her daughter by making the crops wither and the weather cold, creating winter. Hold a Meteorite, symbolizing Demeter's qualities, to help you cope when your own family members are far from home.

Alternative gemstones:
Blood of Isis: Zincite, Cobaltoan Calcite, Mookaite.
Cat's Eye Quartz: Pink Agate, Rose Quartz, Tremolite.
Meteorite: Snowflake Obsidian, Spirit Quartz, Mookaite.

CRYSTALS AND PETS

Just like the human members of your family, your pets can benefit from the amazing power of crystals. If you're getting ready to welcome a new dog or cat into your home, place a Sphene in your living room, which will help to calm any worries or anxieties they might have. If your pet is a rescue animal, they may need extra time to settle, in which case keep a Lithium Quartz nearby to help soothe fears caused by past traumas. Attach a Clear Quartz to their collar to ensure that training goes smoothly.

All dogs can get a little over-excited at times, and the next time yours starts acting up, place a Rainbow Rhyolite somewhere in your home, particularly when you have visitors, to keep your family pet calm.

Finally, Black Tourmaline is a wonderful crystal to use to protect your pets. Keeping this special gem both inside and outside will create a protective aura for your four-legged friends.

BLACK TOURMALINE

Sibling rivalry Replace your envious side with sibling pride by holding a Tourmalinated Quartz by your heart to help you rise above your jealousy, like a rainbow shining through the rain, knowing a pot of gold awaits you elsewhere. **Alternative gemstones:** Datolite, Blue Agate, Spirit Quartz.

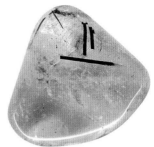

TOURMALINATED QUARTZ

Understanding your parents When our parents give us advice, it isn't because they did things perfectly every time, but because they made mistakes—and learned from them. Write down anything they tell you in a journal, and read through it while holding a Petalite, to ensure that you benefit from their wisdom. **Alternative gemstones:** Ulexite, Barite, Cleavelandite.

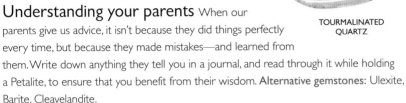

METEORITE

Disorganization at home Keep a Marcasite crystal in your bedroom to improve your organizational skills, and make sure you don't leave the house without your keys and phone ever again! **Alternative gemstones:** Hawk's Eye, Lapis Lazuli, Dumortierite.

ZINCITE

Crystal Fact

Tree Agate is said to help plants grow and is an absolute must for gardeners.

Gardening growth Give your garden a touch of TLC by placing a few Sphene crystals around its borders. Put extra gems in any areas that are looking a bit frazzled to encourage your flowers to bloom, and keep your shrubs looking well groomed. **Alternative gemstones:** Moss Agate, Green Tourmaline, Tree Agate.

COBALTOAN CALCITE

SNOWFLAKE OBSIDIAN

Accepting change A great crystal to use when you're finding it difficult to accept the changes taking place in your life is Apatite. Hold one by your heart to help you welcome, rather than fight against, what's happening, and lessen your fear of the unknown. **Alternative gemstones:** Chrysocolla, Agate, Ajoite.

Crystal Fact

Apatite is said to suppress your appetite and so can help you lose weight.

MARCASITE

CHRYSOCOLLA

DIAMOND

SAPPHIRE

DOLOMITE

ANGELITE

SPIRIT QUARTZ

RHODOCHROSITE

Birthday blues
Fill a photo album with happy memories, and look through it with a Sodalite by your heart any time you start feeling sad about getting older. It will encourage you to remember the smiles behind the lines on your face, and help you to age with grace. **Alternative gemstones:** Diamond, Rhodochrosite, Sapphire.

Enjoying time home alone
"You can never be lonely if you like the person you're alone with." Make these wise words from self-help author and motivational speaker Wayne Dyer your motto by creating a monthly "date night" for me, myself, and I. Tangerose Quartz will remind you that you can be alone without being lonely. **Alternative gemstones:** Pink Halite, Green Phantom Quartz, Chrysoprase.

Show your appreciation
I've spoken to many of the world's best mediums, and the biggest regret of those who've passed is: "I wish I'd shown my loved ones how much I loved them before I left them." Wear a Leopardskin Orbicular Jasper to ensure you don't end up with the same regret. **Alternative gemstones:** Pink Petalite, Yellow Smithsonite, Lemurian Jade.

COPING WITH LOSS

Accepting the death of a loved one is the hardest thing of all. Hold a piece of Morganite by your heart to guide and comfort you through your sorrow, and bring a little lightness to your darkest time.

You can also lessen the pain by wearing a locket containing an image of your loved one together with a Dolomite. The gem will help you to feel closer to the one who's gone, and remind you that your love lives on. A Blue Drusy Quartz beside a photo of your loved one will help, too. Holding the crystal will keep the memories alive in your heart.

After a while, you will be able to turn your sadness into thankfulness for the time you spent together. Wear an Angelite necklace to comfort you through the grieving process, and help you stay strong.

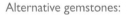

Alternative gemstones:
Morganite: Dolomite, Anhydrite, Spirit Quartz.
Dolomite: Apache Tear, Smoky Quartz, Aqua Aura.
Blue Drusy Quartz: Apache Tear, Smoky Quartz, Amethyst.
Angelite: Aqua Aura, Azurite, Spirit Quartz.

AZURITE

Let the crystals guide you

Add some spice to your daily life by filling a bag with gemstones and picking a different one each week to give yourself a treat. Alternatively, choose a crystal every day for a daily burst of happiness!

Rose Quartz: buy yourself some roses.
Jade: spend time with friends.
Moss Agate: take a nature walk.
Aquamarine: go swimming.
Emerald: spend time with family.
Pink Chalcedony: write a story.

PINK TOURMALINE

Chapter 3
Friendship

Enhance Friendships with the Power of Crystals

True friendships are like the gems in this book—they help us to see our full potential, inspire us to believe anything's possible, and make us feel invincible. But, like crystals, they can be difficult to find, lose their shine, and need recharging from time to time. That doesn't diminish their value though; they can always be revived, rediscovered, or (if necessary) replaced. Whatever the situation, there's a gem to help. Before we go further, here's a quick preview of our next journey together.

If you're hoping to make new friends, go for something blue or green, such as a **Turquoise**, **Bowenite**, or **Blue Opal**, to boost your socializing skills and help you sow the seeds of new friendships. Simply wearing one around your neck or holding it by your throat before a social event or party will help you overcome shyness, insecurity, fear, or any other blocks that are holding you back, and will help you to deepen your connections with others.

Of course, once you've planted those fabulous new friendships, you'll need to water them with lots of love, understanding, and excitement.

Green crystals, including **Jade**, **Emerald**, and **Green Agate**, will take care of the first two, while red and pink gems, particularly **Red Calcite**, **Thulite**, and **Watermelon Tourmaline**, will ensure your social life's full of fun. The red and pink

TURQUOISE

BOWENITE

BLUE OPAL

JADE

EMERALD

THULITE

MAGNETITE

WATERMELON
TOURMALINE

crystals inspire extroversion and are a great help to anyone who is a bit shy as they help you to feel more at ease with other people. **Thulite** is believed to inspire eloquent speech, so if you want to be confident when you're in a crowd of new people, this is the stone for you. **Watermelon Tourmaline** is part of the tourmaline family of crystals, which is closely linked to friendship and a vibrant social circle. Legend has it that tourmaline can be found in all colors because it traveled along the rainbow and gathered all the rainbow's colors as it went. Use a **Tourmaline** to help you gather your own rainbow of fabulous, unique friends.

Sometimes we need to weed out old friendships so new ones can blossom. Gray gems, such as **Tantalite**, **Wind Fossil Agate**, and **Magnetite**, will help you spot the bad seeds in your social circle, and root them out before they cause any lasting damage.

So if you'd like to plant new friendships, water your existing ones, or simply weed out any dried up, toxic, or outgrown ones, this chapter will tell you what to do.

Your Crystal Tips
for Friendship

SARDONYX

PIETERSITE

SMITHSONITE

SCHALENBLENDE

PETALITE

OCEAN JASPER

DALMATIAN STONE

Attract new friends
Draw people to you quicker than a bee to pollen by keeping a Sardonyx crystal in your bag, or placing one near your throat chakra. The crystal will get your social life buzzing in no time, and turn your home into a hive of activity. Alternative gemstones: Turquoise, Danburite, Jade.

Avoiding arguments
As Ghandi once said, "An eye for an eye will only make the world blind." So why waste energy arguing with others, when you can spend it having a ball with them? Wear a Smithsonite necklace to avoid fallouts with friends and loved ones, and help you to see the best in everyone. **Alternative gemstones:** Schalenblende, Green Garnet, Pietersite.

Don't be misled by false friends
Place a Petalite under your pillow to help you find the answers you're seeking within yourself. The gem will empower you to follow, and trust, your own instincts and judgment, rather than relying on a friend who may turn out to be wrong for you. **Alternative gemstones:** Phantom Quartz, Paraiba Tourmaline, Iceland Spar.

Unresolved issues
Wash away past sorrows by writing a letter to the person who hurt you, and placing it under an Ocean Jasper overnight. Throw it into a lake or the ocean the following morning while holding your crystal, and watch it carry away your sadness. **Alternative gemstones:** Petalite, Phantom Quartz, Dalmatian Stone.

Crystal Fact

Turquoise is said to change color if your partner's cheated on you.

THE POWER CRYSTAL: JADE

Astrological sign: Aries, Taurus, Gemini, Libra

Planet: Venus

Element: Earth

Chakra: Heart, Third Eye

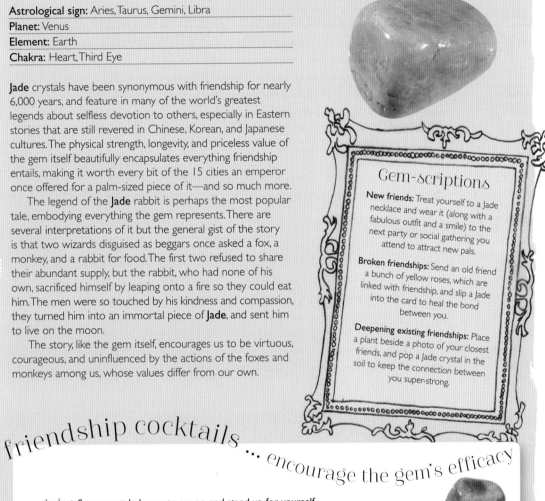

Jade crystals have been synonymous with friendship for nearly 6,000 years, and feature in many of the world's greatest legends about selfless devotion to others, especially in Eastern stories that are still revered in Chinese, Korean, and Japanese cultures. The physical strength, longevity, and priceless value of the gem itself beautifully encapsulates everything friendship entails, making it worth every bit of the 15 cities an emperor once offered for a palm-sized piece of it—and so much more.

The legend of the **Jade** rabbit is perhaps the most popular tale, embodying everything the gem represents. There are several interpretations of it but the general gist of the story is that two wizards disguised as beggars once asked a fox, a monkey, and a rabbit for food. The first two refused to share their abundant supply, but the rabbit, who had none of his own, sacrificed himself by leaping onto a fire so they could eat him. The men were so touched by his kindness and compassion, they turned him into an immortal piece of **Jade**, and sent him to live on the moon.

The story, like the gem itself, encourages us to be virtuous, courageous, and uninfluenced by the actions of the foxes and monkeys among us, whose values differ from our own.

Gem-scriptions

New friends: Treat yourself to a Jade necklace and wear it (along with a fabulous outfit and a smile) to the next party or social gathering you attend to attract new pals.

Broken friendships: Send an old friend a bunch of yellow roses, which are linked with friendship, and slip a Jade into the card to heal the bond between you.

Deepening existing friendships: Place a plant beside a photo of your closest friends, and pop a Jade crystal in the soil to keep the connection between you super-strong.

friendship cocktails ... encourage the gem's efficacy

Jade + Sunstone = help you to say no, and stand up for yourself

Jade + Moss Agate = turn a friendship into a relationship

Jade + Carnelian = remove jealousy between you and your friends

CONFIDENCE BOOSTERS

DANBURITE

The next time your insecurities get the better of you, brush them off gem-style by writing a list of all your accomplishments and placing it in a box with a Crazy Lace Agate. Look at it any time your confidence waivers to boost your self-esteem. You could also write a list of all the amazing friends whom you know want you to be happy and achieve your dreams. Read through the list while holding a Celadonite Phantom Quartz to lift your spirit when you doubt yourself.

If you're especially nervous about an upcoming social event, treat yourself to a Danburite necklace and wear it on the night to maximize your confidence, and attract lots of lovely people your way.

It takes 30 days for a new thought form to become the norm. So do one nerve-wracking thing each day for a month while holding a Dumortierite to turn your insecurity into inner security.

CRAZY LACE AGATE

Alternative gemstones:
Crazy Lace Agate: Okenite, Amethyst, Cerussite.
Celadonite Phantom Quartz: Calcite, Malachite, Beryl.
Danburite: Turquoise, Bowenite, Jade.
Dumortierite: Barite, Opal, Tiger's Eye.

DUMORTIERITE

RED CALCITE

Making new friends
Feeling lonelier than a Fruit Loop in a bowl of Cheerios? Fear not, simply add an Ammolite to your party ensemble and rub it any time you start feeling anxious to maximize your personal charisma and help you make new friends. **Alternative gemstones:** Chrysoprase, Chrysopal, Sardonyx.

NEBULA STONE

Entertaining friends
Turn your social life from silent to vibrant by placing a Red Calcite in your dining room, and throwing a fabulous dinner party for your closest friends. The gem's thought to liven up any social gathering, and will ensure you're at the top of everyone's guest list. **Alternative gemstones:** Pink Crackle Quartz, Turquoise, Danburite.

COVELLITE

GREEN AGATE

BRAZILIANITE

Rekindling friendships True friends are like a good perfume or cologne—fabulous to go out with, great for your self-esteem, and something you feel incomplete without. Send an old friend a photo of the two of you together and a Nebula Stone, to remind you both of the lovely times you shared. **Alternative gemstones:** Diopside, Meteorite, Rose Quartz.

Staying friends Diamonds might be a girl's best friend, but true friends are diamonds, too. Avoid fallouts by placing a Siberian Green Quartz beside a photo of you all together, and looking at it any time your friends annoy you to help you remember how special they are. **Alternative gemstones:** Chrysoberyl, Green Agate, Smithsonite.

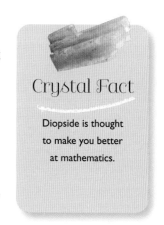

Setting boundaries Self-care is an accessory nobody should be without. Complement yours with a stunning Barite necklace to help you set healthier boundaries with others, and ensure you, and they, don't overstep them. **Alternative gemstones:** Lavender Jade, Brazilianite, Aventurine.

Stay true to your individuality Whoever you are, there's someone, somewhere wishing they were your kind of beautiful. Place a Bronzite crystal near a photo of someone you admire to inspire you to follow your own path in life, and become the person your younger self always hoped you'd be. **Alternative gemstones:** Carnelian, Diamond, Aegrine.

LAPIS LAZULI

Energy vampires A brilliant crystal to use when you feel exhausted by other people's problems is Greenlandite. Wear one around your neck, or hold one by your heart, to prevent your empathy from draining your energy. **Alternative gemstones:** Brazilianite, Cassiterite, Covellite.

Coping with envious friends Hang a Pink Carnelian and evil eye on a string, and place it by your front door to protect you from other people's envy, and ensure any harmful thoughts are seen, sealed, and sent straight back to the sender. **Alternative gemstones:** Red Jasper, Fire Agate, Orange Zircon.

Deepening friendships Strengthen your existing friendships by writing a list of five things you really admire and value about each one while holding a Pink Phantom Quartz by your heart. Send your friends their list out of the blue to remind them how much they mean to you. **Alternative gemstones:** Lapis Lazuli, Emerald, Jade.

THE POWER CRYSTAL: TURQUOISE

Astrological signs: Sagittarius, Scorpio, Pisces

Planets: Jupiter, Venus, Neptune

Elements: Fire, Earth, Air

Chakras: Throat, Brow

Strong yet soothing, **Turquoise** is a stone of protection and healing. The stone's name derives from the French "pierre turquoise," which means "Turkish Stone", because the trade routes used to bring the blue gem to Europe from mines in Asia went through Turkey, and merchants often purchased the gemstone in Turkish bazaars.

Turquoise was sacred to Hathor, the Egyptian goddess of joy and love, and also to the Aztecs and Native Americans. It is a stone of friendship and a perfect gift among friends, as demonstrated by the Arabic proverb: "A turquoise given by a loving hand carries with it happiness and good fortune."

As a symbol of friendship, working with this stunning blue crystal will bring peace to quarreling friends, good fortune to close friends, and protection from negative energies to all friendship groups.

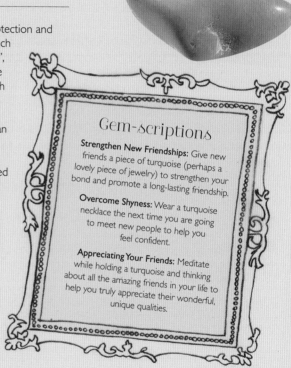

Gem-scriptions

Strengthen New Friendships: Give new friends a piece of turquoise (perhaps a lovely piece of jewelry) to strengthen your bond and promote a long-lasting friendship.

Overcome Shyness: Wear a turquoise necklace the next time you are going to meet new people to help you feel confident.

Appreciating Your Friends: Meditate while holding a turquoise and thinking about all the amazing friends in your life to help you truly appreciate their wonderful, unique qualities.

friendship cocktails ... super-charge your gem

Turquoise + Larimar = bring healing to a damaged friendship

Turquoise + Sodalite = improve communication between friends

Turquoise + Copper = strengthen an existing friendship

RESTORING BROKEN FRIENDSHIPS

Damaged relationships can usually be mended, if the desire is there, and building bridges is a lot better than holding grudges. Write a list of everything you miss about an estranged friend, and read through it with a Schalenblende by your heart. If you feel you can, send it to your friend to open the doors to communication. Otherwise, you could make a friendship bracelet, jazzing up your creation with a Jadeite crystal, and think about the lovely times you've spent together. Pop that in the post, and you'll soon be buddies again!

To make amends for an old quarrel, send your friend some flowers and pop a Navaho Purple Turquoise in the card. Spend five minutes each evening sending them love and kindness, knowing it'll soon lead to rekindled friendship and forgiveness.

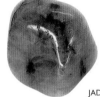

Alternative gemstones
Schalenblende: Diopside, Jasper, Turquoise.
Jadeite: Pink Quartz, Rhodochrosite, Magnesite.
Navaho Purple Turquoise: Jade, Afghanite, Stone of Solidarity.

JADEITE

Spreading happiness among friends
If a + b = c, and a = happy and b = world, what are you left with? That's right, a happy world! Make this your mantra while holding a Spessartite by your heart to inspire you to share your happiness with others.
Alternative gemstones: Citrine, Almandine Garnet, Chrysanthemum Stone.

Achieve harmony in difficult friendships
Struggling to see eye-to-eye with someone? Forget the drama, do the Metta Bhavana! The meditation's a fabulous stress buster, and works even better gem-style. Simply spend five minutes sending your friend love and kindness each day while holding a Faden Quartz to dissolve the tension.
Alternative gemstones: Peridot, Celestite, Siberian Green Quartz.

Turning wishing into reality

We're all capable of doing anything, but nobody can do everything. Turn today's wish list into tomorrow's to-do list by setting yourself little goals each day, and checking them off (with a Wulfenite by your heart) to remind you it's never too late to change your fate. **Alternative gemstones:** Bornite, Bustamite, Cobaltoan Calcite.

Inspiring others

Many of us wish we could go back in time and share the wisdom we now have with our younger selves. Be that person for someone else by wearing a Tanzine Aura Quartz by your heart to turn the weeds of your yesterdays into the seeds of others' brighter days. **Alternative gemstones:** Tugtupite, Ocean Jasper, Lemurian Jade.

Stop gossiping

Better karma comes from avoiding tittle-tattle, no matter how much you may relish any resulting drama. Put a Mohawkite by your phone to remind you not to gossip about others. It will ensure you keep your loose tongue schtum! **Alternative gemstones:** Rose Quartz, Cleavelandite, Atlantasite.

Attracting the right friends

We're all a bit like crystals, each with our own properties that someone, somewhere is looking for. Hold a Zoisite by your heart to ensure you never hide your light but let it shine brightly. The perfect potential friends will be drawn to you, and everyone will accept you. **Alternative gemstones:** Coral, Green Tourmaline, Marcasite.

Have compassion

If our hearts are the sun, our actions are the moon that reflects its light. Hang a sun and moon pendant on a chain together with a Heliodor to inspire you to use your heart and mind to bring light into other people's darkest hours. **Alternative gemstones:** Green Aventurine, Selenite, Spirit Quartz.

HELIODOR

CRYSTALS AND FORGIVENESS

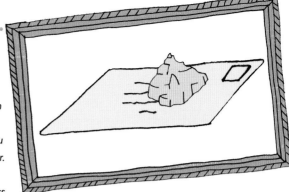

Sometimes we need to forgive others, not because their actions were right, but to free ourselves from the burden of holding on to old grievances. To dissolve your anger and embrace forgiveness is incredibly empowering. If you can do it, you will feel emotionally fit and so much better.

Nelson Mandela once said, "As I walked toward the gate to my freedom, I knew if I didn't leave my bitterness and hate behind, I'd still be in prison." Hold a Pargasite to help you heed his wisdom and free yourself from anger's prison. A piece of Unakite by your heart will also help you to rid yourself of bitterness and forgive those who you feel have wronged you.

Let go of a grudge by holding a Purple Moonstone while writing a letter to the person who has caused these hard feelings. Then throw the letter into the ocean or a lake, knowing that such an action will bring you inner peace; or place it under a Pink Calcite and spend five minutes each night wishing your tormentor well. Your anger will soon lessen.

Buddha tells us that holding onto anger is like grasping a hot coal with the intent of throwing it at someone else—you're the one who gets burned. So Buddhists believe we aren't punished for our anger, but by it. Make this your motto, and hold a Desert Rose to help you forgive those who've hurt you.

If any regrets are holding you back, get rid of them, like a snake shedding its skin. An Onyx crystal over your heart will help, and will also promote forgiveness for the pain others have caused you.

Crystal Fact

Chrysoberyl is thought to help attract a wealthy partner!

Alternative gemstones:

Pargasite: Mohawkite, Khutnohorite, Voescite.
Unakite: Pink Calcite, Chrysoprase, Charoite.
Purple Moonstone: Apache Tear, Sugilite, Chrysoberyl.
Pink Calcite: Citrine, Chrysoprase, Sugilite.
Desert Rose: Diopside, Brandenberg Amethyst, Sugilite.
Onyx: Snowflake Obsidian, Eudialyte, Greenlandite.

EUDIALYTE

PINK CALCITE

ONYX

Guilt from the past Guilt is cruelty's aftertaste, the venom that stings long after the bite itself. Let it go by holding a Pumice and imagining it replacing your scars with bright stars. Then make a wish on one, knowing your wounds will soon dissolve and your guilt shall be absolved. **Alternative gemstones:** Eudialyte, Hackmanite, Hematoid Calcite.

GARNET

Accepting injustice in friendships
Surrender—and put an end to—your suffering by holding an Orange Grossular Garnet by your heart, and asking the universe for courage. Then light a white candle, knowing whatever happens you can handle it. **Alternative gemstones:** Pink Phantom Quartz, Cuprite, Garnet.

Oversensitivity
Guard your sensitivity like the jewels in a treasure chest by holding a Hackmanite over your heart to prevent it from breaking and bruising so easily, and, conversely, to ensure your kindness is not misunderstood. **Alternative gemstones:** Adamite, Aegrine, Alexandrite.

Overreacting
Keep a Creedite in your bag to help you remain calm in any situation. This gem will encourage you to avoid overreacting and help you to stay grounded. **Alternative gemstones:** Brown Zircon, Titanium Quartz, Moonstone.

Compulsive envy
Stop a jealous streak from making you weep by writing a list of five things you're thankful for each day, and placing it, together with a Melanite, in your bag to help you appreciate your blessings and achievements. **Alternative gemstones:** Carnelian, Rose Quartz, Manganoan Calcite.

Help a lonely friend
Loneliness is one of the hardest feelings to endure, but it's very easy to help. Buy a lonely friend, neighbor, or relative a bunch of flowers and slip an Ajo Blue Calcite into the card to heal their sense of isolation. **Alternative gemstones:** Jasper, Cobaltoan Calcite, Uvarovite Garnet.

Forget feeling lonely
We're never alone—not really. At any moment, thousands of characters in books, films, and our imaginations are ready to run away with us. Spend an evening with a mug of cocoa and a Smoky Cathedral Quartz, reading your favorite book to remind you to enjoy time on your own. **Alternative gemstones:** Pink Chalcedony, Almandine Garnet, Sunstone.

Crystal Fact
Alexandrite is thought to make you more graceful and elegant.

Putting yourself out there So many of us wake up each morning, clip our wings together, and then wonder why we can't fly. Locking yourself away from others is the same. Hold a Dream Quartz by your heart to inspire you to spread your wings and fly into the world. **Alternative gemstones:** Danburite, Tugtupite, Strawberry Quartz.

Avoid pessimistic people The next time someone starts raining on your parade, get out your umbrella and walk away. Simply wear a Black Obsidian to prevent other people's gloom from affecting your happiness. **Alternative gemstones:** Aventurine, Red Jasper, Ruby.

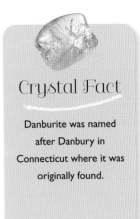

Protect yourself from unkind "friends" Self-help author and motivational speaker Wayne Dyer once compared other people's negativity to a snake bite—it isn't the snake itself, or even the bite, that harms us most, but the venom left behind. Hold a Green Obsidian to prevent the residue of what others say to you from causing you more harm than their original, unkind words. **Alternative gemstones:** Fire Agate, Peach Selenite, Cassiterite.

Backing down too often Sometimes you're given a really awful gift at Christmas, which you feel you have to accept gracefully. Petty squabbles with friends can be like that, but the longer you go on backing down gracefully, the more others will expect you to always accept their point of view. Wear an Atlantasite to help you break the pattern and stick to your own opinion. **Alternative gemstones:** Amblygonite, Bornite, Bustamite.

Accepting hard truths Gems, like friends, can hurt us at times. Some, including Emeralds, reveal different colors when someone's betrayed us, while others, such as Obsidian, bring to light things we don't like. Wear a Graphic Smoky Quartz to help you accept wisdom from friends. **Alternative gemstones:** Sacred Scribe Quartz, Porphyrite, Spider Web Obsidian.

BLACK OBSIDIAN

Overcome resentment The mask of resentment is intended to show others they've been unfair. Then one day we look at our reflection, and realize we are completely trapped by it. Hold a Rhodonite to prevent the scars of the past from becoming a permanent mask. **Alternative gemstones:** Strawberry Quartz, Agate, Rose Quartz.

BARITE

Saying thanks True friendships are like the branches of an ivy plant—they weave together, keep growing taller, and can withstand any weather. Send a Barite to your friends to let them know how happy you are to have them in your life. **Alternative gemstones:** Jade, Turquoise, Watermelon Tourmaline.

BORNITE

ANXIETY TO PLEASE

It's impossible to please everyone and the best advice is to stop trying. A Coral necklace will encourage you to concentrate on satisfying yourself, and Que Sera will help you to overcome your people-pleasing tendencies. Hold one any time someone asks you to do something you'd rather not, take a deep breath, smile politely, and say, "Nope."

Fearing what others think of you is like drinking a shot of tequila—easy to succumb to, bitter to swallow, and unlikely ever to lead to a positive outcome! A Green Calcite crystal next to your heart will stop you from valuing other people's opinions so highly, and holding an Iolite will inspire you to be true to yourself, and resist any toxic behavior you may encounter. Once you decide the only approval you need is your own, you'll be able to follow your own heart. A Cuprite next to it will free you from the burden of other people's expectations.

GREEN CALCITE

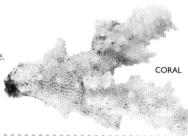

CORAL

Alternative gemstones:
Coral: Muscovite, Topaz, Tourmaline.
Que Sera: Chrysoprase, Snow Quartz, Brazilianite.
Green Calcite: Tourmaline, Coral, Fluorite.
Iolite: Covellite, Blue Topaz, Sodalite.
Cuprite: Pyrophyllite, Zoisite, Iolite.

RHODONITE

Accepting you're wrong
It's never easy to admit that you're in the wrong, but stubbornly refusing to back down in an argument could cost you a wonderful friendship. Hold a piece of Flint as you pick up the phone and call a friend to admit your mistake. **Alternative gemstones:** Dumortierite, Sulfur, Pietersite.

MUSCOVITE

Unite bickering relatives
There was once a goddess called Bridgit who married outside her tribe, and was heartbroken when her son was killed in the ensuing fighting. Her cries were so loud, the families eventually unified. Wear a Jade, which is linked with the goddess, to inspire your family to do the same. **Alternative gemstones:** Pyrolusite, Botswana Agate, Blue Agate.

FLINT

Crystal Fact

Iolites were originally used by Vikings as glasses to protect their eyes from the sun.

Accepting others
Wear a piece of Red Muscovite around your neck to view other people's less attractive traits more compassionately. The gem will prevent you from taking their negative qualities so personally, and stop you from lashing out. **Alternative gemstones:** Rhodonite, Kyanite, Aquamarine.

PINK KUNZITE

Be open-minded Don't dismiss or discount other people or their opinions because they don't always gel with you and yours. Wear a Green Sapphire to encourage you to value other people's special traits.
Alternative gemstones: Chrysoprase, Cleavelandite, Benitoite.

Don't be judgmental Harper Lee's bestselling novel *To Kill A Mockingbird* contains the wise words: "You never really understand a person until you consider things from his point of view … Until you climb inside of his skin and walk around in it." Wear a Green Sapphire to help you see things through other people's eyes, and overcome any prejudice.
Alternative gemstones: Apatite, Chrysopal, Green Jasper.

Crystal Fact

The name "Apatite" comes from a Greek word meaning "to deceive," as the gem is often confused with other crystals.

LETTING GO

Everything changes. Friends can become strangers, and sometimes we need to let go of people, not because we don't love them, but because we love happiness more. Some people are like mountains—overpowering and impossible to see past when you're with them, but smaller and smaller the farther away from them you are. Wear a Tugtupite with Nuummite to help you distance yourself from the mountains in your life.

Albert Einstein defined madness as repeating the same action but expecting a different outcome. Break the cycle by attaching a Selenite to your cell phone to remind you to think twice before making that call to a so-called friend who always brings you down.

A Eudialyte by your heart will help you to walk away from anyone causing you sorrow, and writing a former friend's name on a piece of paper and throwing it into a lake or ocean while holding a Rainbow Aura Quartz by your heart will help you to move on.

Alternative gemstones:
Tugtupite with Nuummite: Citrine, Xenotine, Eudialyte.
Selenite: Elbaite, Charoite, Peridot.
Eudialyte: Pink Kunzite, Rainbow Obsidian, Rainbow Aqua Quartz.
Rainbow Aura Quartz: Rainbow Obsidian, Wind Fossil Agate, Moss Agate.

Chapter 4
Work & Career

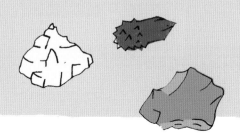

Crystals at Work

So many of us spend our lives looking for a soul mate, not realizing our friends, jobs, and even favorite books can be our soul mates, too. If you find something that really feeds your soul, work no longer seems like work, but is merely following your heart.

Whether you're feeling confused about the path to take, have an important career decision to make, or think the route you've taken is a mistake, the gems in this chapter will help you change your fate. From some super-simple rituals to help you find your perfect vocation to the best gems for dealing with difficult bosses, climbing up the career ladder, and getting a promotion, this chapter's guaranteed to boost your professional luck.

We'll look at ways of helping you overcome any limiting beliefs, such as self-doubt, fear of failure or success, and procrastination, which may be preventing you from following your dreams. **Tiger's Eye**, **Icicle Calcite**, and **Rainbow Rhyolite** are invaluable for this. **Rhyolite** is a stone of change and progress and is really helpful when you need to break out of a career rut! It will light the fire of creativity within your soul and help you to achieve your wildest career ambitions. **Icicle Calcite** is a relatively new addition to the calcite family and was recently discovered in Mexico. It is a powerful crystal that enables you to move forward in your chosen profession without letting fear or self-sabotage hold you back.

We'll also try to work out whether your boss's sexual frustration is the real reason why they treat you like their minion! You'll find tips on the best crystals to use for job interviews, getting a book deal, and helping you stay calm at work. I've also included rituals to help you feel more confident, assertive, and inspired in the office, using **Dendritic Agate**, **Royal Plume Jasper**, and **Poppy Jasper**. The poppy variety of jasper is helpful in spreading cheerfulness and vitality, so use it when your whole office needs a boost of joy! The jasper family of crystals also help you to work harmoniously with others and these are the gems to use when you're struggling to get on with a difficult colleague.

TIGER'S EYE

ICICLE CALCITE

RAINBOW RHYOLITE

JASPER

impress your boss, ace your interviews, and make crystal-clear decisions...

Your Crystal Tips for Work

BLOODSTONE

SUGILITE

PERIDOT

BLUE KYANITE

AMAZONITE

Anger at work
Avoid petty fallouts with colleagues by keeping a Smoky Quartz gemstone on your desk. The gem will surround you in a bubble of positive energy, and help you focus on what you, rather than Janice in IT, should or shouldn't be doing. **Alternative gemstones:** Bloodstone, Sugilite, Blue Kyanite.

Attract new clients
Place a piece of Peridot in your purse or beside some money to wow potential business clients. It's believed to instantly boost your people power, and will magnify your natural charisma. **Alternative gemstones:** Bowenite, Fire Opal, Carnelian.

Communicating with colleagues
Place a Blue Kyanite on your desk to avoid silly squabbles with workmates, and prevent you from losing your temper the next time Mark from accounts starts hassling you again about when you're getting married, starting a family or buying a home. **Alternative gemstones:** Grossularite, Common Opal, Blue Moonstone.

Exam confidence
Ace any exam by keeping a Golden Tiger's Eye crystal in your pocket. Rub it any time your nerves start getting the better of you, and you'll instantly notice your angst lessen. That doesn't mean you can get away with partying till 3a.m. the night before, though! **Alternative gemstones:** Aventurine, Amazonite, Snow Quartz.

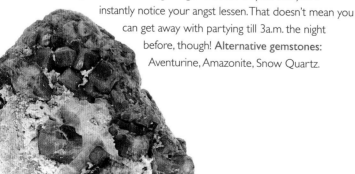

GROSSULARITE

Crystal Fact

Smoky Quartz will not only improve your relationships with colleagues, but also your bank balance, and is an absolute must for shopaholics!

THE POWER CRYSTAL: TIGER'S EYE

Astrological sign: Leo, Capricorn

Planet: Sun

Element: Fire, Earth

Chakra: Solar Plexus, Third Eye

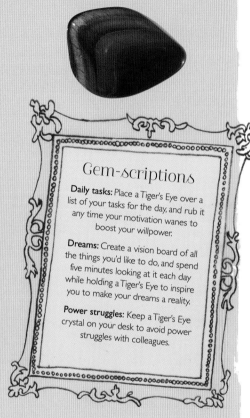

Tiger's Eye crystals have been highly prized since the early 1800s, and continue to mesmerize people with their bewitching powers. Named after the animal whose qualities and symbolism they so beautifully capture, they are the stones for the dreamers, believers, and achievers who have either locked themselves in cages—like tigers in a zoo—or allowed others to put them there. Inspiring us to act rather than dream, **Tiger's Eye** is the zookeeper who comes to set us free.

A stone of integrity, confidence, and courage, **Tiger's Eye** empowers us to walk away from the handmade cage of self-doubt we've built for ourselves, and fulfill our true potential. It encourages us to explore our hidden talents and potential for the first time, and learn how to live by our own rules. The gem is synonymous with career success, inspiring us to focus on our prey, form a strategy for attack, and pounce when the moment's right. Tigers are the largest felines in the world but allow lions to be "kings of the jungle." Likewise, the gem discourages power struggles of all kinds but pushes us to soar, knowing that the "power" we allow others simply gives us more. So, if you're ready to step out of your cage, discover your full potential, and climb to the top of the career mountain, hold a **Tiger's Eye** and prepare to aim for the stars.

Gem-scriptions

Daily tasks: Place a Tiger's Eye over a list of your tasks for the day, and rub it any time your motivation wanes to boost your willpower.

Dreams: Create a vision board of all the things you'd like to do, and spend five minutes looking at it each day while holding a Tiger's Eye to inspire you to make your dreams a reality.

Power struggles: Keep a Tiger's Eye crystal on your desk to avoid power struggles with colleagues.

professional cocktails ... take advantage of opportunities

Tiger's Eye + Citrine = remove fear of responsibility

Tiger's Eye + Blue Lace Agate = help you express your ideas

Tiger's Eye + Agate = find courage to start again

NEW JOB

TIGER'S EYE

SERPENTINE

PICASSO MARBLE

HEMIMORPHITE

HEMATITE

LARVAKITE

SARDONYX

Whether you're just starting out in the world of work or wanting to move on, a new job represents a radical change in your life and so is bound to get the nerves jangling. Calm pre-interview jitters by putting a Black Sapphire crystal under your pillow to ensure you sleep well and are able to do yourself justice. For more of a helping hand, dress to impress by accessorizing your favorite lucky outfit with a Hematite crystal. The gem will strengthen your personal magnetism, and help you blow their socks off! Then, once you've been hired, waltz into your new job without any fear by carrying a Serpentine gem in your wallet or purse. This will help you to hit the professional ground running, and ensure you make a dazzling impression.

Alternative gemstones:

Black Sapphire: Amazonite, Adamite, Magnetite.
Hematite: Zircon, Mookaite, Adamite.
Serpentine: Yellow Tourmaline, Blue Sapphire, Cinnabar.

Thinking big Forget thinking outside the box—break out of it altogether by holding a Stone of Dreams to help you live each day as if it's your last, and ensure you don't leave the world with your music, or any regrets, still inside you. **Alternative gemstones:** Bronzite, Tiger's Eye, Fire Opal.

Taking action There's only one place where progress comes before work and that's in the dictionary! So stop dreaming and start scheming by placing a Jasper crystal in your office to help you get your projects out of your head, and into the world. **Alternative gemstones:** Septarian, Diamond, Tiger's Eye.

Completing projects Stick to your projects like icing on a cupcake by placing a Hemimorphite on your desk to help you stay motivated, and prevent you from giving up before the recipe for your success is fully baked and served to perfection. **Alternative gemstones:** Honey Calcite, Picasso Marble, Red Chalcedony.

Motivation Keep your drive sky high by spending five minutes holding a Poppy Jasper each morning. Visualize all the fabulous things your project will lead to, and your enthusiasm will soon know no bounds. and help you manifest your dreams. **Alternative gemstones:** Sardonyx, Tiger's Eye, Larvakite.

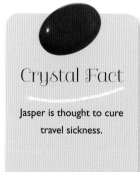

Crystal Fact

Jasper is thought to cure travel sickness.

Empowerment

Think like a boss and earn lots of dosh by placing a Dendritic Agate beside your business cards, or anything with your name on it. Rub it any time you feel anxious for an instant confidence boost. **Alternative gemstones:** Amethyst, Cinnabar, Carnelian.

Dealing with setbacks at work

Marilyn Monroe was once told she had no future in showbusiness. Did she give up? Hell, no! Handle any rejections Marilyn-style by wearing a pendant with the word "dream" and a Halite around your neck to prevent you from giving up on yours, however much you're tested. **Alternative gemstones:** Cleavelandite, Cassiterite, Cobaltoan Calcite.

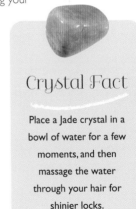

ORANGE CALCITE

Boosting energy

Swap your daily latte fix for energetic bliss by creating your own emergency vitality kit. For an instant pick-me-up, simply rub some cayenne essence on a piece of fabric, pop it in a pouch with an Orange Jade, and hold it any time your get-up-and-go wanes. **Alternative gemstones:** Fire Opal, Orange Calcite, Golden Topaz.

Envy at work

Hold a Hematoid Calcite to help you release (rather than unleash) your envy the next time a less-qualified/younger/generally annoying colleague gets the promotion/raise/recognition you deserve. **Alternative gemstones:** Blue Kyanite, Apatite, Petrified Wood.

Professional guilt

We all want to be super-successful, and that can mean sacrificing parts of our personal lives for our professional ones. Make sure you get the balance right by placing a Merlinite under your pillow to help you find the perfect way to dance your way to the top. **Alternative gemstones:** Ulexite, Zircon, Mookaite.

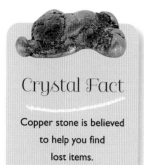

Crystal Fact

Copper stone is believed to help you find lost items.

Crystal Fact

Aquamarines are thought to cure seasickness.

Crystal Fact

Chalcedony, particularly the pink variety, is said to boost your story-telling skills and is a great crystal for writers.

Impatience More restless than an espresso-loving woodpecker? Keep calm and carry a Copper Stone! The gem will stop you from being so fidgety, and introduce you to someone you might not be familiar with—Master Patience, which is exactly what it will help you to do. **Alternative gemstones:** Danburite, Watermelon Tourmaline, Emerald.

Harmony at work Replace office rivalry with friendly camaraderie by treating your colleagues to a new indoor plant and slipping a Chalcedony behind it to help everyone get along better, and create a kind and loving atmosphere. **Alternative gemstones:** Spirit Quartz, Yellow Fluorite, Sandstone.

Judging others Everyone you meet, however confident, cheerful, or successful, is fighting their own battle. Wear a Lepidocrosite by your heart to remind you to be careful with the words you choose, as one day you could be walking in their shoes. **Alternative gemstones:** Chrysoprase, Aquamarine, Metamorphosis Quartz.

Becoming the boss Any time you start doubting your ability to be in charge, look at yourself in the mirror while holding a Royal Plume Jasper, and affirm, in the words of Joan of Arc, "I'm not afraid. I was born to do this." Then go out there and do yourself justice. **Alternative gemstones:** Pyrite, Aventurine, Onyx.

Starting a new business Create lots of interest in your new venture by slipping a Red Chalcedony into your accounts book or cash register. This will help your business get off the ground, and quickly turn those dimes into dollars. **Alternative gemstones:** Citrine, Carnelian, Adamite.

Workaholics Make sure you know when to switch off by keeping a Green Jasper by your front door to prevent you from taking your work home with you, and ensure your profession doesn't become an obsession. **Alternative gemstones:** Almandine Garnet, Merlinite, Yellow Apatite.

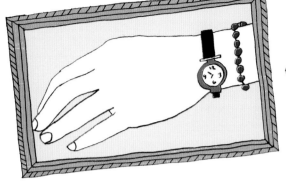

Time management

There are 24 hours in a day, and everyone—from a pilot who flies to 10 different countries, to a server who waits on 300 people—has exactly the same amount of time. Wear a Staurolite bracelet beside your watch to inspire you to tick off your tasks each day as it ticks away the minutes. **Alternative gemstones:** Morganite, Lapis Lazuli, Rainforest Rhyolite.

Selling skills Amaze prospective buyers with your magical ability to sell and make sure they fall under your spell by wearing an African Jade necklace to maximize your natural charisma, and make you luckier than a four-leaf clover. **Alternative gemstones:** Cinnabar, Thulite, Golden Topaz.

Spreading good feeling at work "There are two ways of spreading the light; to be the candle, or the mirror that reflects it." Make writer Edith Wharton's wise words your motto by doing a daily act of kindness. Hold a Blue Phantom Quartz and know that your good deeds are sowing the seeds of other people's happiness. **Alternative gemstones:** Cerussite, Chalcedony, Chrysanthemum Stone.

Compassion at work Everyone we meet teaches us something, and the ones who hurt us most are often our best teachers. Spend five minutes thanking them for the lessons they taught you, while holding a Morganite with Azeztulite, to help you see the gain in the pain they inflicted on you. **Alternative gemstones:** Chrysoberyl, Tektite, Sunstone.

SANDSTONE

ALMANDINE

MORGANITE

AFRICAN JADE

CINNABAR

CERUSSITE

TEKTITE

Setting boundaries at work

They say what you resist persists, but what you accept others expect, too. Hold an Anthrophyllite by your heart to prevent people from taking advantage of your kindness, and ensure that saying yes to them doesn't mean saying no to yourself. **Alternative gemstones:** Barite, Brazilianite, Pyrophyllite.

The wisdom of experience

They say a picture's worth a thousand words, we each have a canvas of colorful tales inside us—some sketchy, others surreal, and a few highlighting our own or other people's poor traits. Hold a Wind Fossil Agate to inspire you to learn from the art in your heart. **Alternative gemstones:** Jade, Beryl, Celestite.

DEALING WITH NEGATIVITY

There's nothing more annoying than someone saying you can't do something, and nothing more gratifying than listening to what they say and doing it anyway! Holding a Rutilated Kunzite will prevent other people's negativity from bringing you down. Alternatively, pop on your headphones, hold an Aqua Aura, and play your favorite happy song. It will drown out their negativity (literally!), and ensure you keep dancing on the inside, no matter what's happening around you.

Alternative gemstones:
Rutilated Kunzite: Trummer Jasper, Tree Agate, Silver Leaf Jasper.
Aqua Aura: Blue Tourmaline, Aventurine, Diamond

Crystal Fact

Aqua Aura is believed to keep your fruit and vegetables fresher.

Enthusiasm for learning new skills
Knowledge is power, and something you can always acquire and develop. Write a list of five things you'd like to know about, and spend 15 minutes reading about each one, with a Purple Fluorite close by, to reawaken your passion for learning. **Alternative gemstones:** Snow Quartz, Dalmatian Stone, Aquamarine.

ICELAND SPAR

Learning from others
There are more than seven billion people in the world, and every single one of them knows something you don't. Start a wisdom journal, and write down anything enlightening that others tell you. Read through it while holding an Iceland Spar, to enrich your vision with their wisdom. **Alternative gemstone:** Lepidolite, Galena, Hiddenite.

HIDDENITE

Work stress
Prevent your job from taking its toll by doing this super-simple breathing exercise, while holding a Blue Jade, any time you start feeling stressed. Close your eyes, put your hands on your heart, and inhale for eight counts (and out for the same) to help you stay sane. **Alternative gemstones:** Golden Topaz, Fire Opal, Beryl.

AZURITE

Overcome indecisiveness
Hold an Azurite crystal to help you view your choices more objectively, and give you the courage to trust your own judgment. **Alternative gemstones:** Rutilated Quartz, Green Tourmaline, Ruby.

SARDONYX

Deal with holding-back syndrome
There are between 25,000 and 30,000 days in the average lifetime and "someday" isn't one of them, so stop waiting and start creating by placing a Tiger's Eye over your bucket list to help you seize the day—today! **Alternative gemstones:** Sardonyx, Red Calcite, Golden Topaz.

GOETHITE

Achieve crystal-clear thinking
Hold a White Calcite gemstone to your forehead any time your mind gets fuzzy. It's like having your very own internal housekeeper, and will ensure your inner world's as spick and span as your outer one. **Alternative gemstones:** Celestite, Pink Opal, Morganite.

GALENA

Learn from your mistakes
Turn errors into opportunities to grow by placing a Cobalto Calcite under your pillow to prevent you from blaming yourself or others for what happened, and empower you to recognize the lessons it taught you. **Alternative gemstones:** Peacock Ore, Goethite, Blue Aragonite.

WHITE CALCITE

Go your own way

To paraphrase playwright and critic George Bernard Shaw: life isn't about finding yourself, but creating your (best) self. Follow his advice by wearing a Metamorphosis Quartz around your neck to help you shape your own destiny, find your ideal career, and write the perfect ending to your hand-made fairytale. **Alternative gemstones:** Goshenite, Shattuckite, Blue Sapphire.

GOSHENITE

METAMORPHOSIS QUARTZ

Uncertainty at work

Hold a Tanzanite by your heart to clear away any clouds, such as other people's opinions, which may be preventing you from sharing your light with the world. It will free your heart to shine through, like the sun, and help you see your destiny. **Alternative gemstones:** Stibnite, Lodestone, Sugilite.

SHATTUCKITE

Be open to new knowledge

People can accuse you of many things in life— talking too much, not talking enough, eating too much, not eating enough (you get the idea!)—but no one can ever criticize you for being too smart. Hold a Pink Chalcedony to reawaken your passion for learning. **Alternative gemstones:** Aquamarine, Citrine, Carnelian.

TANZANITE

Express your talents

As spiritual teacher and writer Marianne Williamson once said, "There's nothing enlightened about shrinking so others won't feel insecure around you." Shine bright, like a Diamond, by wearing one around your neck to inspire you to share your light with the world. **Alternative gemstones:** Astrophyllite, Yellow Topaz, Marcasite.

CARNELIAN

Learning from difficult experiences

Pearls are produced when a parasite enters an oyster's body and is covered with layers of a shimmering substance known as nacre until it's no longer a threat. Wear a Blue Holly Agate around your neck to inspire you to make something beautiful from your own difficult times. **Alternative gemstones:** Jade, Zircon, Sapphire.

DIAMOND

Dealing with workplace bullies

We're all born with our own superpower—the love in our hearts. But, like any superhero, there are times when we need to protect ourselves from other people's kryptonite. Hold a Winchite gemstone to help you rise above petty office bullies. **Alternative gemstones:** Beryl, Limonite, Yellow Labradorite.

LODESTONE

FLUORITE

LABRADORITE

Focus on the task at hand Feeling as unfocused as a broken satnav? Hold a Sillimanite while you're meditating to prevent your mind from wandering, and ensure you aren't thinking about what's for dinner when you should be focusing on your breathing! **Alternative gemstones:** Fluorite, Quartz Crystal, Labradorite.

Embracing change The next time you're feeling anxious about a work-related change of some kind—perhaps you're taking on more responsibility, or a new manager is joining your team—place a Madagascar Cloudy Quartz in a box and decorate it with inspiring pictures from your morning paper to remind you that a change really can do you good. **Alternative gemstones:** Moonstone, Chiastolite, Crocoite.

Moving on from setbacks Imagine what would happen if the sun gave up every time its light was blocked by a cloud—we'd be in darkness forever! We need to think about our setbacks in the same way. Hang a sun pendant on a chain with a Chohua Jasper to inspire you to rise again after your rainy days. **Alternative gemstones:** Agate, Danburite, Hematite.

CHIASTOLITE

DANBURITE

GOLDEN CALCITE

LACK OF CONFIDENCE

Everyone knows that self-doubt is an obstacle to be overcome on the way to success, but that doesn't mean that confidence comes easily, although it can easily take a knock. When your faith in yourself needs a boost, wear a piece of Golden Calcite around your neck to help you see how gifted and worthy of success you are, and remember the words of former First Lady Eleanor Roosevelt—"No one can make you feel inferior without your consent." Wearing a Stichtite and Serpentine will help to boost your self-perception, and remind you that you are just as good as anyone else.

The only difference between victim and victor is perception. As Buddha said, "what you think, you become," so, in other words, to be a champion you must think like one. Put your victim mentality to rest by holding a Realgar and Orpiment by your chest; and should the occasion arise when you've just got to be so utterly fabulous that no one can knock you, hold an Epidote in Quartz, affirm that you are utterly fabulous, and kick out any mental block that's stopping you from forging ahead.

Alternative gemstones:
Golden Calcite: Chrysoberyl, Manganoan Calcite, Pink Kunzite.
Stichtite and Serpentine: Yellow Jasper, Garnet, Lavender-Pink Smithsonite.
Realgar and Orpiment: Lapis Lazuli, Tourmaline, Snow Quartz.
Epidote in Quartz: Quantum Quattro, Smithsonite, Angelite.

STICHTITE

ANGELITE

CHRYSOBERYL

SERPENTINE

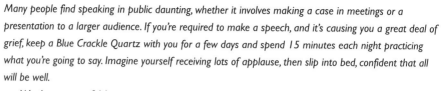

SPEAKING TO A CROWD

Many people find speaking in public daunting, whether it involves making a case in meetings or a presentation to a larger audience. If you're required to make a speech, and it's causing you a great deal of grief, keep a Blue Crackle Quartz with you for a few days and spend 15 minutes each night practicing what you're going to say. Imagine yourself receiving lots of applause, then slip into bed, confident that all will be well.

PYRITE

Words are powerful, but sometimes at work our voices are drowned out by louder colleagues. If having your say at meetings is a challenge, due to more forceful speakers or your lack of confidence, do a mini-visualization beforehand. Simply hold a Green Agate gemstone and imagine yourself performing brilliantly. Take the gem into the meeting with you, and smile as you make your points. Wearing a Dendritic Chalcedony will help you make yourself heard and allow you to shine.

EPIDOTE

Alternative gemstones:
Blue Crackle Quartz: Blue Apatite, Blue Kyanite, Turquoise.
Green Agate: Sodalite, Amethyst, Celestite.
Dendritic Chalcedony: Bronzite, Stromatolite, Purpurite.

STRAWBERRY
QUARTZ

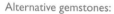

Break out of your comfort zone

If you continue to do what you've always done, you'll stop yourself from becoming the best you can become. Place a Pyrite in Quartz beside a globe to help you break out of your comfort zone, and ensure you don't confuse what's comfortable with what's possible. **Alternative gemstones:** Morganite, Strawberry Quartz, Garnet.

GREEN AGATE

MORGANITE

Taking a gamble
If no one took risks, nothing could ever have been discovered! Nurture your inner adventurer by holding a Poldervaarite to help you seize the day, every day! **Alternative gemstones:** Thulite, Peach Aventurine, Heulandite.

Bad day in the office
It doesn't matter how spiritual you are, working life can be tough and some days will leave you reeling. Survive those occasions by throwing yourself a pity party, complete with chocolates, sad music, the lot! Keep a Maw Sit Sit nearby, and your self-pity will soon run dry. **Alternative gemstones:** Epidote, Jasper, Carnelian.

THE POWER CRYSTAL: JASPER

Astrological sign: Leo
Planet: Sun, Mars
Element: Fire
Chakra: Base

Mysterious and captivating, **Jasper** is famous for its ability to protect and instill confidence and courage in its owner. Historically, **Jasper** has been considered a sacred and powerful stone by all ancient peoples and civilizations.

The red variety of the stone is particularly helpful for those who work in the performing arts as this gem helps them to become more sensitive to their audiences.

Jasper can be used in all industries. It acts as a professional support for those in jobs requiring strength and stamina, such as police officers. This crystal also brings energy and alertness to workers who must focus intensely on the task at hand, such as doctors.

Wearing a piece of **Jasper** jewelry will help you to keep calm during stressful times at work, and it will also promote harmony among you and your colleagues. Use this balancing stone to help you achieve your career goals and be successful, whatever your job.

Gem-scriptions

Give Confident Presentations: Overcome nerves about public speaking by wearing an item of Jasper jewelry on the day of your presentation.

Stop Procrastinating: Keep a piece of Jasper on your desk to ensure you stay focused and work through your to-do list in super-quick time.

Deal with Negative Colleagues: Hold a piece of Jasper when speaking to a grumpy colleague to prevent their negativity from affecting your mood.

career cocktails ... take advantage of opportunities

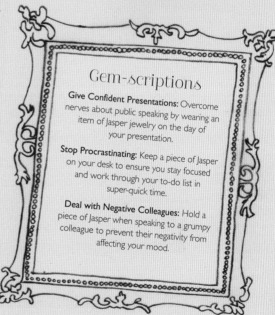

Jasper + Amethyst = create positive energy in the workplace

Jasper + Lilac Lepidolite = banish work stress

Jasper + Merlinite = find the perfect work-life balance

Waiting for feedback
Standing by for reactions is never easy, but the law of attraction can help, and works even better gem-style. Simply hold a Carrollite and imagine the best possible outcome to ensure your nerves stay in check, and you hear what you expect. **Alternative gemstones:** Golden Beryl, Prophecy Stone, Lodolite Quartz.

Work-related nightmares
Given that most of us spend approximately 2,080 hours at work each year, it's hardly surprising if professional stress affects our daily rest. Place a Richterite under your pillow to prevent tomorrow's spreadsheets from disturbing tonight's sleep. **Alternative gemstones:** Brazilianite, Strawberry Quartz, Verdelite.

Criticism
We all love gifts, and the more we're given, the greater the chances we'll find something we can use. It's the same with criticism, which doesn't have to be negative. Write down any criticism you receive and hold a Kunzite to help you read between the lines and see the gifts in what you find. **Alternative gemstones:** Sunstone, Fire Opal, Cassiterite.

Rise to the challenge
Sticks and stones might break our bones, but look at all the wonderful things we can make from them! We can use sticks to warm and adorn our homes, and gemstones for almost anything. Wear an Orange Grossular Garnet to turn what could break you into a breakthrough. **Alternative gemstones:** Sugilite, Sardonyx, Ruby.

Dealing with difficult people
"We don't see things as they are, but as we are." And if writer Anaïs Nin's words are true, other people's perceptions are reflections of them rather than us. Hold an Iridescent Pyrite by your heart to prevent other people's issues from affecting you. **Alternative gemstones:** Tugtupite, Spectrolite, Rhodonite.

BRONZITE

KUNZITE

RUBY

CASSITERITE

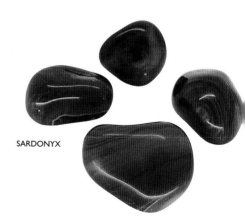

SARDONYX

Raise your expectations

Michelangelo is alleged to have said, "Our greatest danger isn't setting our aim too high and falling short, but setting it too low and achieving our mark." Wear a White Sapphire to inspire you to aim for the moon, knowing you'll still shine like a star whether or not you get that far. **Alternative gemstones:** Zincite, Imperial Topaz, Blue Topaz.

Accepting help

Everything in nature relies on something else to survive—trees need rain to grow, the moon needs the sun's glow, and even gemstones need to be discovered. Wear a Porphory to help you accept that everything and everyone—including you—needs help sometimes. **Alternative gemstones:** Tangerine Quartz, Topaz, Rose Quartz.

ZINCITE

Seizing new opportunities

When a knock comes at our door, it's usually for a good reason—a chance to see someone we're missing, gain knowledge or wisdom, or face something we've been trying to ignore. Wear a Peach Aventurine to ensure you answer when opportunity comes knocking. **Alternative gemstones:** Icicle Calcite, Orange Calcite, Okenite.

Spotting new opportunities

Self-help author and motivational speaker Wayne Dyer tells us that "when you change the way you look at things, the things you look at begin to change." And it's true. Wear a Kornerupine to help you notice the blooms rather than thorns on every flowering bush, and the new possibilities that open up every day. **Alternative gemstones:** Watermelon Tourmaline, Muscovite, Sapphire.

IMPERIAL TOPAZ

Changing direction

A man walked down a road and straight into a puddle. The next day, he took the same road, walked around the puddle, but stumbled and stepped in. On the third day, he took a different road. Hold a Stichtite to prevent you from walking into the same puddles time and time again. **Alternative gemstones:** Chrysoberyl, Charoite, Moonstone.

TANGERINE QUARTZ

Believe there are no ill winds

We all make mistakes and an Onyx will help to you see that every cloud has a silver lining. Hold one of these beautiful stones to help you see the upside of your mistakes. **Alternative gemstones:** Snowflake Obsidian, Eudialyte, Wind Fossil Agate.

ROSE QUARTZ

ORANGE CALCITE

Office politics They say money's the root of all evil, and when people are competing for the same high-paid promotion, or trying to impress the boss, office life can become tense and stressful. Place a Schalenblende beside a vase of white tulips in your office—the flowers represent forgiveness and fresh starts—to weed out any rivalry and restore harmony. **Alternative gemstones:** Flint, Grossularite, Calcite Fairy Stone.

Witty response The next time your boss puts you on the spot, dazzle them with your humor and razor-sharp wit by keeping a Watermelon Tourmaline in your pocket to help your confidence soar sky high. **Alternative gemstones:** Goethite, Pyromorphite, Snakeskin Agate.

Cure stress quickly Stress is never welcome, so give your mind a rest by rubbing or holding a Gabbro over your third eye, which is located in the middle of the forehead. This will help your anxiety disappear. **Alternative gemstones:** Schorl, Aquamarine, Blue Quartz.

Under pressure Singer-songwriter Bob Marley once said, "Sometimes you don't know how strong you are until being strong is your only choice." And he was right. The harder the fight, the stronger you become. Hold a Lemurian Jade by your heart to help you to stay strong. **Alternative gemstones:** Black Agate, Adamite, Wind Fossil Agate.

Crystal Fact

Dreams about Diamonds are thought to predict recognition from high places.

Crystal Fact

Sunstone will give you the motivation to stick to your exercise regimes.

Crystal Fact

The name "Selenite" comes from the Greek word "selenites," meaning "stone of the moon."

ACCEPTING SUCCESS

Sometimes you've got to forget what you think and remember what you deserve. Denying yourself success because you don't believe you deserve it is like the moon refusing to shine because the light isn't its own. When all's said and done, some of the world's light is gone. Wearing a Hematite will help you to enjoy your success, and any time you start doubting your right to it, hold a Golden Calcite, look at your reflection, and affirm, "I deserve nothing less than perfection."

Sometimes the root of the problem is that we're afraid to succeed. As spiritual teacher and writer Marianne Williamson said, "Our deepest fear is not that we're inadequate, but powerful beyond measure: it's our light not our darkness that most frightens us." Remember this, while holding an Icicle Calcite, whenever you're in danger of standing in front of your own sunlight.

SCAPOLITE

PYROMORPHITE

Alternative gemstones:
Hematite: Scapolite, Tourmalinated Quartz, Larimar.
Golden Calcite: Sunstone, Green Calcite, Spirit Quartz.
Icicle Calcite: Sunstone, Yellow Topaz, Spirit Quartz.

BLACK AGATE

Perseverance Walt Disney was once fired for having "no imagination," Elvis Presley was told he'd be better off driving a truck than performing, and Van Gogh sold one painting in his lifetime! Wear a Stromatolite to inspire you to stand tall, and keep going in the face of adversity. **Alternative gemstones:** Que Sera, Zircon, Selenite.

APOPHYLLITE

Accepting authority Nobody likes being told what to do, but our line managers and bosses are just doing their job and trying to make things run smoothly. Wear a Greenlandite bracelet to remind you that a bit of authority in the system helps everybody. **Alternative gemstones:** Smithsonite, Ruby, Aventurine.

HESSONITE

Feeling unappreciated Power isn't about being the loudest. Characters in books can influence us more than anyone we ever meet without even a peep. Keep an Iron Pyrite beside your favorite novel, and hold it any time you start feeling invisible at work to help you realize your potential and stand out from the crowd. **Alternative gemstones:** Hessonite Garnet, Eosphorite, Stichtite and Serpentine.

Doing yourself justice There's a sweet sadness about evening primrose flowers—they keep their beautiful scent locked away all day, only releasing it at night. Treat yourself to some of these beautiful blooms, and keep them beside a Chrysanthemum Stone to inspire you to spread your heavenly scent as you were meant to do. **Alternative gemstones:** Apophyllite, Diamond, Stichtite.

Be ambitious Helen Keller, deafblind author, political activist, and lecturer, once said, "The only thing worse than being blind is having sight but no vision." Place a Vivianite over your eyes to help you heed her wisdom and prevent you from limiting your ambition. **Alternative gemstones:** Jade, Leopardskin Jasper, Idocrase.

SEPTARIAN

Inspire your team More than 2,500 years ago, Buddha sat under a tree, reached enlightenment, and started a spiritual revolution. One person's vision can inspire generations. Keep a picture of Buddha on your desk beside a Green Selenite to ensure you inspire everyone you work with. **Alternative gemstones:** Aquamarine, Fuchsite, Septarian.

A new career

It can be difficult to select a new career path, so let the crystals guide you. Visit a crystal store and see if you are drawn to any of the following stones, which all indicate a new direction.

Rose Quartz: writer or artist.
Citrine: retail or teaching.
Tourmaline: starting a business.
Apatite: healing.
Tiger's Eye: accounting or police work.
Green Moss Agate: gardening or farming.
Pink Tourmaline: politics.

A difficult boss

Let the crystals give you guidance when you're struggling with a tricky boss. Pick a gem at random to help you fathom why your boss is giving you a hard time. Remember that, even though they're at the top of the career foodchain, your boss still has a job to do and they have their own stresses to deal with.

CHRYSOPRASE

MELANITE

Overcome ageism Success has nothing to do with age, so don't think that you won't get that promotion just because you're a bit older or younger than your colleagues. Wear Petrified Wood to ensure the lines on your face don't interfere with your pace in the work place. **Alternative gemstones:** Pink Crackle Quartz, White Opal, Youngite.

VIVIANITE

Getting a promotion Everyone starts from the bottom. Jennifer Aniston was once a waitress, Madonna worked in a donut shop, and Julia Roberts used to sell ice cream! Place a Snakeskin Pyrite beside a picture of one of these fabulous ladies, or someone else you look up to, to inspire you to rise to the top like they did. **Alternative gemstones:** Adamite, Tree Agate, Hematite.

IDOCRASE

PETRIFIED WOOD

The gems below show you some of the hidden problems that could be causing tension between you and your boss.

Hematite: fear of failure.
Melanite: jealousy.
Muscovite: insecurity (either theirs or yours.)
Gold: inferiority complex.
Imperial Topaz: stress.
Chrysoprase: sexual frustration!

GOLD

Next career move

Why go to a psychic when you've got hundreds of gem advisers? Open this book at random, and the gem you're most drawn to on the page will help you gauge your next career stage.

Moss Agate: pay rise or promotion.
Black Sapphire: new job.
Ruby: more power.
Ocean Jasper: more responsibility.
Hematite: new opportunity.
Snow Quartz: big changes.

Chapter 5
Abundance

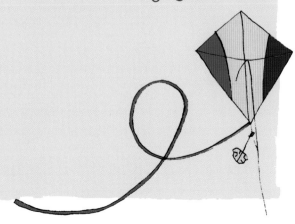

Crystals to Attract Abundance

While money might not seem like a very spiritual subject, let's be honest, we all need it, and it's good to be grateful for our material blessings.

In this chapter, we'll look at ways to help you attract, maintain, and maximize prosperity, and work on busting through any negative beliefs, such as unworthiness, guilt, or toxic habits, that may be sabotaging your relationship with money.

However, with so many gems to choose from, it can be hard to remember what does what, so I've come up with a super-simple way of helping you recall the best colors to turn to—simply think about their traits, and something they create.

CITRINE

For instance, yellow and gold crystals, such as **Citrine**, **Yellow Sapphire**, and **Gold**, are the same color as the sun, which brings us light, so these can be used to bring money into our lives. **Gold** in particular has long been associated with power, wealth, and prosperity. The ancient Egyptians

GOLD

thought **Gold** was the symbol of the powerful sun god, Ra, while the Incas thought it was the sweat of the sun (and silver was formed from the tears of the moon). Green stones, such as **Green Tourmaline**, **Moss Agate**, and **Tree Agate,** are the same color as grass, which grows, so these can help our finances grow. **Moss Agate** has historical links with abundance and has been closely connected to agriculture, with medieval farmers believing that using the gem while a crop was planted would lead to a strong and healthy yield. We can use the stone today to ensure our financial endeavors produce similarly spectacular results!

GREEN TOURMALINE

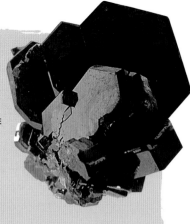

VANADINITE

Then, of course, there are the red and gray crystals, such as **Vanadinite** and **Smoky Quartz**. These are the colors of fire and smoke, which harm our health, so they prevent us from harming our wealth.

We'll also look at ways of helping you win competitions, attract new clients to your business, and even pass your driving test!

So whether you're hoping to break up with your toxic beliefs about money, rebuild something you've lost, or start a new and healthier relationship with your finances, this chapter will ensure you and your bank balance live wealth-ily ever after.

MOSS AGATE

TREE AGATE

SMOKY QUARTZ

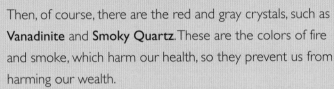

Boost your finances with powerful citrine and gold...

Your Crystal Tips
for Abundance and Prosperity

Improve your finances Nurture your finances by putting a Tree Agate in a flowerpot with your favorite plant. The gem will maximize your cash flow, and ensure your bank balance and plant continue to blossom. **Alternative gemstones:** Epidote, Emerald, Green Moss Agate.

Creating abundance Become your own money-making genie by placing a piece of Cinnabar in your savings box to multiply your existing income, and guarantee you're never short of cash-raising ideas. **Alternative gemstones:** Malachite, Green Tourmaline, Tiger's Eye.

GREEN MOSS AGATE

Change your luck Stop feeling unlucky and start earning lots of money by slipping an Adamite in your mailbox to help you climb the professional ladder with amazing speed and dexterity. **Alternative gemstones:** Cinnabar, Black Sapphire, Serpentine.

Anxiety about money A brilliant stone to use when you're feeling anxious about your finances is Jade. Place it by your heart to overcome any negative beliefs or self-destructive patterns that may be affecting your relationship with money. **Alternative gemstones:** Peridot, Green Calcite, Citrine.

Avoid overspending An absolute must for shopaholics is Vanadinite. Take one on your next shopping spree to prevent any excessive splash-outs. **Alternative gemstones:** Smoky Quartz, Green Quartz, Green Spinel.

THE POWER CRYSTAL: CITRINE

Astrological sign: Aries, Gemini, Leo, Libra

Planets: Sun and Jupiter

Element: Air

Chakra: All

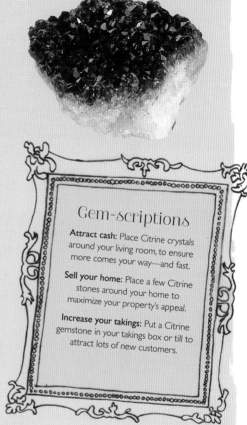

Citrine crystals are the working-class heroes of the gem world. Associated with abundance, prosperity, and wealth from as far back as 280 BCE, the stone is actually one of the least expensive to purchase, and often thought of as the "poor man's topaz."

Known as "the merchant's stone," it encourages us to aim for the big things, and appreciate the small ones, and has been placed in people's cash registers and pockets for centuries to attract and maintain abundance. The gem inspires us to invest in our greatest asset—our minds—with confidence, self-belief, and optimism, ensuring any negative savings we've accumulated, such as self-doubt, fear, and unworthiness, are swiftly dispersed.

Citrine is a teacher, motivator, and life coach in a gemstone. It supports us through any doubts about our worth by reminding us what we deserve. If you think you're unworthy, this beautiful crystal will help you unravel your hand-woven story, and show you that the future's yours for the taking and your dreams are still there waiting.

The gem inspires us to shape our own destinies. It encourages us to recognize that we can't win the lottery without buying a ticket, get our dream job without applying for it, or reach the top of the ladder if we haven't stepped on it.

Gem-scriptions

Attract cash: Place Citrine crystals around your living room, to ensure more comes your way—and fast.

Sell your home: Place a few Citrine stones around your home to maximize your property's appeal.

Increase your takings: Put a Citrine gemstone in your takings box or till to attract lots of new customers.

cash cocktails ... double your manifesting powers

Citrine + Smoky Quartz = prevent overspending

Citrine + Morganite = attract love

Citrine + Emerald = heal family rifts

Attracting abundance

Keep a Citrine gemstone in your purse, wallet, or beside some money to increase your financial success. It will boost your money-making mojo, and turn you into an instant cash magnet. **Alternative gemstones:** Jade, Jet, Yellow Sapphire.

Changing fortunes

Wear a Chrysopal by your heart to embrace any changes that are taking place in your life, even if you need to take a little time to adjust to them. Flowering shrubs may lose their blossoms but they soon bloom again, and you too will soon brighten up the world again with your beauty. **Alternative gemstones:** Crocoite, Eudialyte, Iolite.

Be financially successful

Keep a Yellow Jasper in your purse to help you maximize your financial luck. The gem is guaranteed to attract lots of money your way, and will have you splashing the cash in no time. **Alternative gemstones:** Citrine, Aventurine, Cinnabar.

For general good fortune

Swap feeling unlucky for being happy by keeping a Cat's Eye in your bag, or wearing one around your neck. It's luckier than any horseshoe, and will ensure everything you touch turns to gold. **Alternative gemstones:** Sardonyx, Copper, Staurolite.

Prosper in a new venture

Give your new venture some tender loving nurture by placing a Jet in your cash box or purse to help you set the business's wheels in motion, and ensure it quickly becomes a money-making sensation. **Alternative gemstones:** Peridot, Pyrite, Jade.

Be optimistic

Forget settling for a glass half-full attitude to life. Fill that cup to overflowing by spending five minutes each morning dancing to your favorite happy song while holding a Star Sapphire to keep your optimism at its optimum. **Alternative gemstones:** Moonstone, Muscovite, Blue Chalcedony.

Crystal Fact

Citrine might be great for your finances, but it can turn you into a terrible gossip too!

BLUE CHALCEDONY

Count your blessings

Adopt a "la vie en rose" (French for "life in pink") view of the world by wearing a Rainbow Obsidian around your neck to help you see and appreciate the beauty in everything, however challenging. **Alternative gemstones:** Sapphire, Turquoise, Tree Agate.

WULFENITE

Dreaming big

They say the sky's the limit, yet men have flown to the moon; and in the driest of deserts flowers can bloom. Hang a Nirvana Quartz on a flower pendant to encourage you to see the possible in every impossible, and ensure your dreams come true. **Alternative gemstones:** Astrophyllite, Bustamite, Aqua Aura, Spirit Quartz.

Changing the world

Follow Gandhi's example and "be the change you wish to see in the world." Make this your mantra by writing it on a piece of paper and reading through it with an Ambygonite by your heart to encourage you to be, and see, the kindness in mankind. **Alternative gemstones:** Bornite, Calcite Fairy Stone, Diopside.

The power of kindness

Showing kindness is often mistaken for weakness, but it's actually an incredible strength. Hold a Tremolite to help you remember that niceness is always good and can even lift others with its strength. **Alternative gemstones:** Sodalite, Amethyst, Okenite.

Gratitude for the present

Every day might not be wonderful, but there's always something wonderful in each one. Make this your motto by writing down everything you're thankful for each evening while holding a Lemurian Jade to help you turn your bad days into awe-filled ones. **Alternative gemstones:** Dendritic Chalcedony, Snakeskin Agate, Alexandrite.

Contentment

Life can be a lot like a game of cards—we meet diamonds, jokers, and knights or queens who steal our hearts, and definitely have moments when we'd like to "snap." Wear a Shell Jasper to help you feel content with the hand you have been dealt. **Alternative gemstones:** Wulfenite, Halite, Covellite.

Cultivate enthusiasm

The word enthusiasm comes from the Greek term "enthousiasmos," meaning the "God within." Hold a Blue Topaz by your heart to inspire you to follow your dreams and embrace your destiny. **Alternative gemstones:** Bustamite, Yellow Topaz, Aegrine.

BLUE TOPAZ

Rebuilding happiness

As poet, writer, and philosopher Ralph Waldo Emerson said, "Happiness is a perfume you can't pour on others without getting on yourself." Heed his words by doing a random act of kindness every day for a week, and holding a list of your deeds and a Sapphire any time your sparkle fades. **Alternative gemstones:** Cobaltoan Calcite, Turquoise, Tree Agate.

SAPPHIRE

Moving on

It's never too late to start again. At any moment, one hello, goodbye, or one last try could give you the courage to make overdue changes. Hold a Steatite by your heart to help you embrace any new chapter in your life. **Alternative gemstones:** Red Jasper, Black-Banded Agate, Snakeskin Agate.

RED JASPER

Gratitude for the self

Turn your "can'ts" into "cans" and your inner critic into a fan by holding an Almandine Garnet, and adding 15 minutes of "me time" to your day. The gem will encourage you to be kinder to yourself, and empower you to nurture, rather than torture, your soul's rapture. **Alternative gemstones:** Pink Crackle Quartz, Pink Danburite, Strawberry Quartz.

ALMANDINE

Gratitude for the past

Right now, you're wiser than you've ever been. Celebrate this by writing your sorrows on a piece of paper, and the lessons they taught you on another. Burn the first while holding a Goethite and watch as your past burns to oblivion, leaving you with only its wisdom. **Alternative gemstones:** Wind Fossil Agate, Cleavelandite, Creedite.

GOETHITE

Manifesting your dreams

Any idea you conceive, you can achieve. Affirm this to yourself daily by writing your wish on a piece of card and reading through it with a Bastnasite by your heart. This will help your wish to be swiftly manifested. **Alternative gemstones:** Red Chalcedony, Smoky Quartz, Cassiterite.

JET

Manifesting money

Spend five minutes each night holding a Yttrian Fluorite and imagining your financial dreams coming true. Then hand over your request to the universe, knowing your vision will soon become a reality. **Alternative gemstones:** Green Tourmaline, Citrine, Jet.

GREEN TOURMALINE

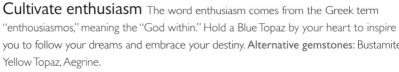

CASSITERITE

Crystal Fact

Topaz is linked to
generosity and can also
be used to cleanse, heal,
and balance the emotions.

Crystal Fact

Moonstone is said to
help you through
the menopause.

Crystal Fact

The name "Citrine"
comes from the French
word "citron,"
meaning "lemon."

Trust in the power of the universe We never doubt that the sun will rise each day, and earth will keep spinning along, yet we question whether or not the universe will manifest our dreams. Hold a Catlinite to strengthen your faith in the universe. **Alternative gemstones:** Variscite, Topaz, Blue Quartz.

Don't give up Feeling powerless doesn't mean you have no power, but simply less power than before. Affirm this to yourself by placing a Serpentine in Obsidian beside a photo of someone you admire to remind you that one pebble can spread ripples across an entire ocean. **Alternative gemstones:** Sunstone, Smoky Amethyst, Tanzanite.

Self-improvement Turn to the trees! They're definitely the best teachers of all. They show us how to give without taking, bend without breaking, and grow while remaining grounded. Sit beside one while holding an Elestial Quartz to turn its wisdom into your life's mission. **Alternative gemstones:** Tourmaline, Amazonite, Moonstone.

Follow your dreams Our dreams are like kites—we can release them into the world, or hold on to them with all our might. Hold a Pyrite with Sphalerite to empower you to live and love as though you've never been pulled down, and dream with your eyes wide open. **Alternative gemstones:** Bustamite, Ruby, Icicle Calcite.

GOOD FORTUNE

Most get-rich-quick schemes are doomed to failure but if you put your faith in crystals, you have a good chance of your financial prayers being swiftly answered. Golden Topaz speeds up any attempt to attract good fortune, so a piece of Golden Topaz jewelry is an appealing option.

Quartz in Gold is another gem to consider. According to the Law of Attraction, what we think, we attract. So if you want more money, you need to start thinking that you're already rich! Simply read through a catalog while holding a Quartz in Gold and circle the things you'd like to have. Place the gem by some cash and await events.

If winning some cash is on your agenda, give Lady Luck a helping hand by placing a piece of Green Aventurine in your left pocket to magnify your winning potential. Who knows, you may even hit the jackpot!

Alternative gemstones:
Golden Topaz: Golden Apatite, Peridot, Green Calcite.
Quartz in Gold: Citrine, Jet, Yellow Sapphire.
Green Aventurine: Jade, Goldstone, Spiral Green.

ALEXANDRITE

STIBNITE

TURQUOISE

IOLITE

UNAKITE

MOONSTONE

The power of reinvention
There are times in life when we can sit back and wait for the storms to pass, or put on our wellies, grab our umbrellas, and dance in the rain. Hold an Arfvedsonite by your heart to help you reinvent your outlook on life. **Alternative gemstones:** Alexandrite, Snakeskin Agate, Muscovite.

Get published
When I was 13, I read Roald Dahl's *Matilda*, turned to my mother, and said, "I'm going to be a writer." And here I am today! Create an ideas journal, and autograph it. Read through it with a Valentinite and Stibnite each night, knowing a book deal will soon be in sight. **Alternative gemstones:** Citrine, Turquoise, Blue Topaz.

You deserve happiness
"Ever since happiness heard your name, it's been running through the streets trying to find you." The poet Hafiz spoke the truth—whoever you are, and whatever you've been through, happiness belongs to you. Hold a Yellow Scapolite to help you believe that. **Alternative gemstones:** Celadonite Quartz, Chrysoprase, Rose Aura Quartz.

Crystal Fact

Muscovite will give you clear and sparkly eyes.

Appreciating the present moment

People often say that an angel sits on one of our shoulders, and a devil on the other. I believe that two devils sit on our shoulders, the past and the future, and an angel—the present—resides in our hearts. Hold an Infinite Stone to prevent the past or future from casting a shadow over your present. **Alternative gemstones:** Unakite, Iolite, Pink Petalite.

Find your winning streak

According to legend, Alexander the Great's 11-year winning streak was due to the Chrysoprase crystal he kept in his girdle. He's thought to have lost the gem one day while bathing, and never won another battle. Carry one with you as a lucky talisman. **Alternative gemstone:** Mohawkite, Actinolite, Agrellite.

Be thankful for small blessings

There was once a pelican who became so captivated by the Opals he saw, he began pecking at them. The sparks soon turned to flames and spread to a nearby camp, allowing its residents to cook for the first time. Hold one to help you appreciate life's smaller blessings. **Alternative gemstones:** Nebula Stone, Tangerine Quartz, Poppy Jasper.

Pass that driving test

Curb driving-test nerves by wearing an Orange Zircon necklace, or keeping one in your pocket, to help you overcome your anxiety and worry. **Alternative gemstones:** Moonstone, Turquoise, Aventurine.

Teaching others

Everything changes, but the footprints we leave in other people's hearts never disappear. Hold a Boli Stone and post online a list of lessons you've learned to ensure your wisdom lives on. **Alternative gemstones:** Diopside, Amblygonite, Annabergite.

Crystal Fact

Chrysoprase is believed to make you more graceful.

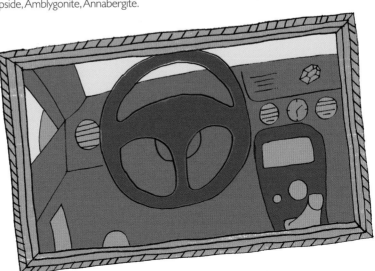

Chapter 6
Health & Wellbeing

Crystals for Health and Wellbeing

MAGNESITE

MUSCOVITE

ALEXANDRITE

AMETHYST

BERYL

Crystals have been used to inspire and enhance beauty for centuries; from legends about Egyptian queens grinding **Lapis Lazuli** stones into powder and using it as eye shadow, to stories about Roman women dying their hair the color of amber to appear more youthful, gems are the embodiment of health and wellbeing.

In this chapter, we'll work on perfuming your soul with positivity, rinsing your mind with confidence, and bathing your heart in self-love.

We'll cleanse, tone, and moisturize your thinking habits with **Magnesite**, **Muscovite**, and **Alexandrite**, to boost your confidence and help you kick out any toxic beliefs; and ensure you never go to bed wearing the day's stressful make-up again by using **Amethyst**, **Beryl**, and **Chrysoprase** to help you wipe away your tension, and get your beauty sleep. **Beryl** was an ancient cure for hiccups! The patient would drink a **Beryl**-infused elixir to get rid of the troublesome hiccoughing. Today, the gem is still used in its elixir form as a gargle to cure throat infections.

Enhance your inner (and outer!) beauty with the power of crystals...

We'll also work on making sure you start each day with a hearty bowl of optimism, mug of energy, and slice of willpower, using **Black Tourmaline**, **Aquamarine**, and **Ruby**, and help you blitz any last-minute zits or stubborn wobbly bits with **Rose Quartz** and **Snowflake Obsidian**. According to Greek mythology, **Aquamarine** belonged to the seductive Sirens and was washed ashore when it spilled from their jewelry boxes. Sailors then wore the stone as an amulet to protect them from the Sirens' call and to ensure they had a safe voyage at sea.

There are also tips on the must-have gems to keep in your make-up bag for on-the-spot top-ups of memory, courage, and happiness, using **Howlite**, **Chiastolite**, and **Blue Euclase**, as well as advice on the best crystals for weight-loss, anti-aging, and nights out with friends.

So if you're ready to shape up your thinking, detox your beliefs, and give your mind, body, and soul a spiritual makeover, read on to give yourself the x-factor!

CHIASTOLITE

CHRYSOPRASE

AQUAMARINE

Your Crystal Tips
for Health and Wellbeing

Complexion Perfection Boost your complexion by placing a Rose Quartz crystal in your bath water. It's like all your favorite pampering essentials combined in a gemstone, and will leave you looking and feeling wonderful. **Alternative gemstones:** Jade, Tanzanite, Almandine.

Detoxing Start your purifying regime by keeping a Snowflake Obsidian by your fridge to help you make wiser food choices, and prevent you from raiding the cookie jar! **Alternative gemstones:** Pink-Banded Agate, Ruby, Chlorite.

PINK-BANDED
AGATE

Enhancing beauty Rub a piece of Amber on your skin to bring out your natural beauty. It's an absolute must for nights out with friends, and will turn you into an instant object of desire. **Alternative gemstones:** Aquamarine, Spinel, Imperial Topaz.

Wrinkle-busting Feeling wrinklier than a prune? Defy the laws of aging by placing an Opal crystal in your tub to improve your skin's elasticity, and leave you looking as smooth as a fresh plum. **Alternative gemstones:** Sapphire, Moonstone, Pearl.

Crystal Fact

Pearl is thought drastically to reduce menstrual cramps.

THE POWER CRYSTAL: OPAL

Astrological sign: Cancer, Libra, Scorpio, Pisces
Planet: Venus
Element: Water
Chakra: Heart, Throat, Crown (varies according to color)

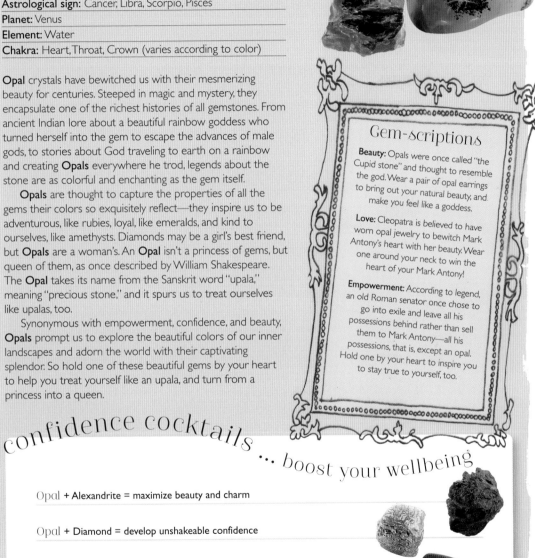

Opal crystals have bewitched us with their mesmerizing beauty for centuries. Steeped in magic and mystery, they encapsulate one of the richest histories of all gemstones. From ancient Indian lore about a beautiful rainbow goddess who turned herself into the gem to escape the advances of male gods, to stories about God traveling to earth on a rainbow and creating **Opals** everywhere he trod, legends about the stone are as colorful and enchanting as the gem itself.

Opals are thought to capture the properties of all the gems their colors so exquisitely reflect—they inspire us to be adventurous, like rubies, loyal, like emeralds, and kind to ourselves, like amethysts. Diamonds may be a girl's best friend, but **Opals** are a woman's. An **Opal** isn't a princess of gems, but queen of them, as once described by William Shakespeare. The **Opal** takes its name from the Sanskrit word "upala," meaning "precious stone," and it spurs us to treat ourselves like upalas, too.

Synonymous with empowerment, confidence, and beauty, **Opals** prompt us to explore the beautiful colors of our inner landscapes and adorn the world with their captivating splendor. So hold one of these beautiful gems by your heart to help you treat yourself like an upala, and turn from a princess into a queen.

Gem-scriptions

Beauty: Opals were once called "the Cupid stone" and thought to resemble the god. Wear a pair of opal earrings to bring out your natural beauty, and make you feel like a goddess.

Love: Cleopatra is believed to have worn opal jewelry to bewitch Mark Antony's heart with her beauty. Wear one around your neck to win the heart of your Mark Antony!

Empowerment: According to legend, an old Roman senator once chose to go into exile and leave all his possessions behind rather than sell them to Mark Antony—all his possessions, that is, except an opal. Hold one by your heart to inspire you to stay true to yourself, too.

confidence cocktails ... boost your wellbeing

Opal + Alexandrite = maximize beauty and charm

Opal + Diamond = develop unshakeable confidence

Opal + Red Jasper = witness transformation

Be body confident

Boost your body image by placing a Magnesite crystal and a notebook on your bedside table. Write down five things you like about yourself each morning, and keep the gem and journal with you all day. Your confidence will soon sky-rocket! **Alternative gemstones:** Vanadinite, Chrysoprase, Rhodochrosonite.

Appreciate your beauty

Turn your body image from drab to fab by placing a Muscovite crystal on your bedside table to silence the negative voices within, and help you realize how gorgeous you are. **Alternative gemstones:** Carnelian, Jade, Magnesite.

Quietening racing thoughts

When you're finding it difficult to silence the voices within, Beryl is a brilliant crystal to use. Put one under your pillow to clear and quieten your mind, and help you to stop stressing. **Alternative gemstones:** Pink Opal, Rhomboid Calcite, Yellow Labradorite.

Insomnia

Swap counting sheep for blissful sleep by creating your own dream pillow. Pop some dried lavender buds and an Amethyst on to a piece of fabric, tie it together, and place it inside your pillow. Then snuggle into bed, shut your eyes, and say goodbye to sleepless nights forever. **Alternative gemstones:** Hematite, Chrysoprase, Lapis Lazuli.

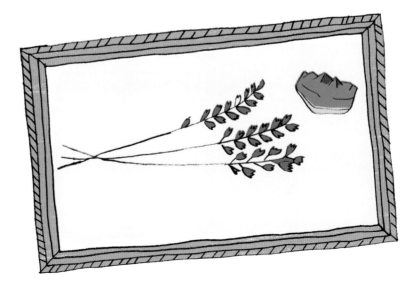

RESTORING GOOD HUMOR

Life has its ups and downs and the trick is to get over the downs as quickly as possible. Any time you start feeling weary or sad, wear something blue, the color associated with peace and tranquility. Complement your outfit with a Blue Euclase to go from feeling worn down to relaxed in a jiffy.

If you're just feeling flatter than a yoga mat, the thing to do is to create your own DIY spa by lighting some candles, running a bubble bath, and placing an Aquamarine on the side of your tub to revitalize your energy and ensure your worries go down the drain along with your bath water. But when life really turns sour, look for Chiastolite. Wear one around your neck to brighten your outlook on life, and help you turn the bitterest of lemons into the sweetest of cupcakes—with a cherry on top!

Alternative gemstones:
Blue Euclase: Jasper, Quartz, Calcite.
Aquamarine: Pink Sunstone, Carnelian, Poppy Jasper.
Chiastolite: Sapphire, Azeztulite, Okenite.

VANADINITE

HOWLITE

Improve your memory
More forgetful than a goldfish with amnesia? Place a piece of Howlite on your third eye to boost your memory skills, and ensure you don't forget Aunt Deirdre's birthday again. **Alternative gemstones:** Rhodonite, Tourmaline, Emerald.

AZEZTULITE

Balance your mood
Feeling pricklier than a cactus? Keep a Pearl in your pocket, and rub it any time someone gets your back up to help you stay grounded, and prevent you from throwing a hissy fit. **Alternative gemstones:** Chalcedony, Prehnite, Aquamarine.

OKENITE

Being alone
Feel gratitude for times of solitude by making a date with yourself (and an Ice Quartz) each week, and treating yourself to a meal, movie, or box of your favorite chocolates. Keep the gem with you, and hold it any time you feel lonely to remind you of the spiritual plenitude of moments spent in solitude. **Alternative gemstones:** Pink Phantom Quartz, Cobaltoan Calcite, Pearl Spa Dolomite.

RHODONITE

Crystal Fact

Sapphire is thought to make you smarter.

Find inner strength
We can learn a lot from sunflowers—they don't wait for the sun's rays to find them, but turn around to face them. Hold an Anthophyllite to inspire you to look for the sunlight wherever you go and whatever circumstances you find yourself in. **Alternative gemstones:** Cinnabar Jasper, Garnet, Sunstone.

CHALCEDONY

SUNSTONE

MOOKAITE

UNAKITE

SERAPHINITE

AMETRINE

VERDELITE

LARIMAR

Weight loss

A brilliant crystal to use when you're hoping to lose weight is Mookaite. Place one by your secret snacking stash to avoid any late-night chocolate binges. **Alternative gemstones:** Unakite, Seraphinite, Quartz.

Face challenges calmly

Wear a Green Opalite necklace, or hold one by your heart, to help you stay strong when things go awry, and encourage you to be heartened by the challenges life throws at you, but never made insensitive by them. **Alternative gemstones:** Dendritic Agate, Ametrine, Emerald.

Accepting your feelings

Our emotions can be like the ocean—reflecting the sun's light during our soul's summer, and absorbing the world's tears when the heavens open. Hang a Verdelite on a yin-yang necklace to help you accept the natural tides of your mind. **Alternative gemstones:** Gray-Banded Agate, Pumice, Brazilianite.

Heal your heart

Wear the ultimate heart healer, Chrysoberyl, around your neck to overcome any toxic thinking patterns that are causing you pain. **Alternative gemstones:** Larimar, Pink Tourmaline, Hemimorphite.

Breaking bad habits

Give your willpower a boost by writing a list of five reasons why you'd be happier, healthier, and better off without your habit, and placing it under an Alexandrite. Look at it any time your determination wanes to help you stay strong. **Alternative gemstones:** Ruby, Peridot, Black Onyx.

Instant pick-me-up

When life gets tough, pick yourself up by walking away from the drama, and saying a mantra. Find a Black Tourmaline, look in a mirror, and say, "Hakuna matata," which is Swahili for "no worries." You should straight away feel calmer. **Alternative gemstones:** Black Agate, Adamite, Jade.

Stay happy at work

If happiness is the aim, kindness is the game. Affirm this to yourself daily by writing down a number of mini-treats on separate pieces of paper and popping them in a jar. Pick one for yourself each day, and wear a Pink Danburite as you do it, to remind yourself that merry memories begin with "'me." **Alternative gemstones:** Manganoan Calcite, Rose Quartz, Chrysoprase.

Look after yourself
Sometimes we really are our own worst enemies! We work too hard, we don't sleep enough, and we worry about unimportant things. Hold a Drusy Golden Healer Quartz to ensure your inner warrior, rather than worrier, takes the lead in your life. **Alternative gemstones:** Chrysoprase, Rose Quartz, Chrysoberyl.

No regrets
Holding onto the past is a futile exercise and only saps your energy. Place a Calcite Fairy Stone by your heart to help you remember that those "if onlys" still could be. **Alternative gemstones:** Blood of Isis, Icicle Calcite, Cassiterite.

Silencing mind chatter
The next time your mind's feeling busier than an interstate during rush hour, hold a Rhomboid Calcite and picture yourself sitting beside the ocean. Imagine the waves calming your spirit and washing away the commotion of the day. You'll soon feel peaceful again. **Alternative gemstones:** Rhodozite, Vanadinite, Snow Quartz.

Prevent a bad night's sleep
There are no two ways about it—sleepless nights are an absolute no-no. Hold a Blue Calcite over your third eye, or keep one with you for an hour or so before bed, to help you and your mind unwind and prepare for rest. **Alternative gemstones:** Amazonite, Tourmaline, Pink Opal.

Instant power boost
Strength isn't about size. The smallest crystal can have a powerful healing effect. That's the great thing about gems—you don't even need to touch them to be touched by them. Hold a Super 7 (and this book) to remind you there are hundreds of gems you can turn to. **Alternative gemstones:** Rose Quartz, Jasper, Okenite.

Fresh starts
Hold a Red Jasper gemstone to help you emerge from any difficulty, like a caterpillar leaving its cocoon to become a butterfly, ready to spread your wings, and start a new phase in your life. **Alternative gemstones:** Spinel, Charoite, Chiastolite.

Crystal Fact

The name "Garnet" is thought to come from the Latin word "granatus," meaning "pomegranate," due to the gem's resemblance to the fruit's seeds.

Have daily zest

Pick a gem and say a mantra to add some pep to everyday life. Here are a few ideas.

Strawberry Quartz: I love myself wholeheartedly.
Morganite: I embrace others open-mindedly.
Red Garnet: I'm hot.
Rose Quartz: I deserve perfection.
Pink Halite: I'm surrounded by affection.
Pink Crackle Quartz: My best friend is me, something I hope you'll all be saying, and truly believing, by the end of this book.

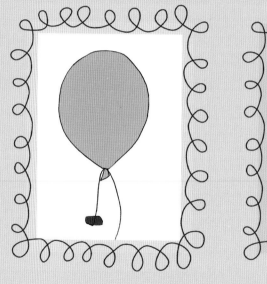

Chapter 7
Mind, Body, Spirit

Crystals for the Mind, Body, and Spirit

PINK KUNZITE

BLUE KYANITE

For centuries, people believed that **Pearls** were the moon's tears, **Opals** were created from a bolt of lightning thrown at a rainbow by a Greek god, and **Diamonds** were the tears of gods. Crystals, as you can see, are as sacred and powerful as we perceive them to be—and so are we.

While the crystals in this chapter might not instantly make you see yourself as a god or goddess, they will help you to value your potential as something sacred, like a crystal.

We'll go through all the colors of a rainbow and more—from pink gems, including **Pink Aura Quartz**, **Pink Danburite**, and **Pink Kunzite**, which will help you to realize how wonderful you are, to blue crystals, such as **Blue Lace Agate**, **Larimar**, and **Indicolite**, which will ensure you let others see that, too. **Blue Lace Agate** will help you to communicate clearly and speak your truth, particularly in situations where you need to stand up for yourself. The gem will allow other people to see your truly unique and amazing qualities.

We'll also look at ways to help you overcome any guilt, self-limiting beliefs, or past mistakes that are holding you back, using **Voegesite**, **Astrophyllite**, and **Snowflake Obsidian**, and work on filling your mind with so much self-love, positivity, and happiness there simply won't be room for anything negative.

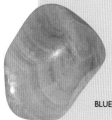

BLUE LACE AGATE

TURQUOISE

There are also tips to help you overcome your fears, insecurities, and effects of past relationships, as well as advice on how to boost your singing, writing, and karaoke skills, using **Turquoise**, **Carnelian,** and **Blue Kyanite**. As a member of the kyanite family, **Blue Kyanite** has a powerful energy that allows you to break through creative blockages and rediscover your creativity. **Carnelian** is another high-energy stone that will restore your motivation if you are feeling low. It will help you to make your dreams become a reality.

As we move toward the end of our journey together, I hope you'll take heed and learn self-worth, so you can look in the mirror, smile at your beautiful reflection, and wholeheartedly say, "Yes, I am as special as a god/goddess, and deserve nothing less than the very best."

INDICOLITE

SNOWFLAKE
OBSIDIAN

CARNELIAN

develop intuition, overcome self-doubt, and unlock your creativity...

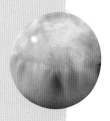
LARIMAR

Your Crystal Tips
for Mind, Body, and Spirit

CHRYSOPRASE

STICHTITE

EUDIALYTE

CHAROITE

FIRE AGATE

Self-acceptance Holding a Chrysoprase crystal is like having the support of everyone you love in a gem stone. Place it by your heart to help you cherish, appreciate, and accept yourself as much as your closest friends do, and chase away your inner fears. **Alternative gemstones:** Stichtite, Pink Kunzite, Eudialyte.

Overcoming fear Awaken the hero within by holding a Larimar crystal whenever you're feeling anxious about something in particular. It will help give you the courage to embrace what you're afraid of, and empower you to feel the fear and do it anyway! **Alternative gemstones:** Citrine, Charoite, Hematite.

Rise above judgment Crystals of Red Tourmaline were confused with rubies for centuries before the green variety caught Tiffany & Co.'s eye in 1876. Wear one to help you stay true to yourself, regardless of what others say about you, knowing your real worth will be recognized by those who matter. **Alternative gemstone:** Coral, Fire Agate, Green Calcite.

Appreciate your unique qualities As Buddha tells us, "All of us, as much as anyone, deserve our own love and affection." Heed his wisdom by holding a Thulite gemstone by your heart to help you appreciate your own gifts and beauty. **Alternative gemstones:** Titanium Quartz, Obsidian, Larimar.

Aimlessness Feeling a little lost? Every evening, take a 15-minute walk, carrying a Lapis Lazuli with you, and think about the five things you most enjoyed doing at work. Repeat the ritual every evening, and keep the gem with you all day. You'll soon know where your heart lies. **Alternative gemstones:** Barite, Thulite, Titanium Quartz.

THULITE

THE POWER CRYSTAL: AMETHYST

Astrological sign: Virgo, Capricorn, Aquarius, Pisces
Planet: Jupiter, Neptune
Element: Air, Water
Chakras: Crown, Brow

The name **"Amethyst"** comes from the Greek word "amethystos," meaning "not intoxicated," which is exactly what the gem does for us. Whether our vision of reality is being distorted through a feeding frenzy of toxic relationships, thoughts, and beliefs, or others are spiking our minds with a lethal cocktail of anger, bitterness, and self-doubt, **Amethyst** is the wise friend telling us we've had enough, and are ready to go home.

The gem even protects us while we sleep—either literally by guarding us from negative energies and intruders during the night, or by appearing in our dreams, even if we don't own a crystal ourselves, to assure us we'll soon be free from harm.

The stone's history alone is enough to leave you feeling intoxicated with power. From legends about Cleopatra's magical **Amethyst** ring, which could capture the heart of any man, including Julius Caesar and Mark Antony, to stories about Egypt's wealthy kings and queens giving the gem to the poorer people, it's impossible not to be seduced by the crystal's legacy.

Teaching us how to feel rich without being rich, love without someone to love, and unite rather than fight, Amethyst is the matchmaker that brings our hearts and minds together, and ensures nothing comes between them.

Gem-scriptions

Protection: Place an Amethyst crystal by your front door, or hang one on a windchime by your window, to protect you and your loved ones from negative energy.

Nightmares: Put an Amethyst stone under your pillow or on your bedside table to scare away bad dreams.

Toxic thinking: Start a compliments journal, and write down anything nice anyone says to you. Read through it with an Amethyst by your heart to remind you how wonderful you are.

happiness cocktails ... enhance your self-worth

Amethyst + **Green Aventurine = protect yourself from overly demanding friends**

Amethyst + **Pink Crackle Quartz = boost self-image**

Amethyst + **Smoky Quartz = stop yourself falling back into bad habits/relationships**

DREAMS

We all dream but remembering them is another matter. Wouldn't it be wonderful if we could experience fully, and savor, each and every moment of our lifetime, whether waking or sleeping? However, that requires us not only to remember our dreams but to understand and interpret them, too—all a bit of a tall order, but, as ever, crystals can help.

A Prehnite placed over your third eye before bedtime will help you to recall everything from your nightly escapades, aided by a Malachite under your pillow. Keep a pen and notebook by your bed, and write down everything you remember in the morning. Repeat the process each day, and you'll soon realize what your heart is telling you. Alternatively, it may be that your dreams have another meaning. In the same way that everyone we meet teaches us something, many dreams have messages to bring and can provide answers if we are seeking guidance. Keep an Andalusite under your pillow, and record everything you remember to help you unravel the riddles in your night-time wanderings, or a Molybdenite to come up with the advice you need.

Of course, not all dreams are good ones and no one wants to encourage nightmares. A Celestite crystal on your bedside table has the effect of an angel watching over you while you sleep, so that the only thing giving you a fright is your alarm in the morning! If a bad dream does manage to creep through, try this super-simple ritual. It's a fabulous pick-me-up for mornings after bad dreams. Place a Clinohumite in your bathroom, jump in the shower, and imagine the water washing away the night's terror. You'll soon feel peachy again. Avoidance is better than cure, though, so to dispense with night-time terrors and turn yourself into a keen, serene dreaming machine, keep a Green Opal crystal with you all day. It'll awaken (pun intended!) your imagination, and make sure your sleeping world is as fabulous as your waking one.

Alternative gemstones:

Prehnite: Red Jasper, Mookaite, Poppy Jasper.
Malachite: Larvakite, Kyanite, Smoky Quartz.
Andalusite: Boulder Opal, Picasso Marble, Smoky Quartz.
Celestite: Gold, Ruby, Manganoan Calcite.
Clinohumite: Lepidolite, Copper, Peridot.
Green Opal: Jade, Moldavite, Spirit Quartz.
Molybdenite: Shaman Quartz, Adamite, Fenster Quartz.

MALACHITE

BOULDER OPAL

CELESTITE

MOLDAVITE

LEPIDOLITE

GREEN OPAL

ADAMITE

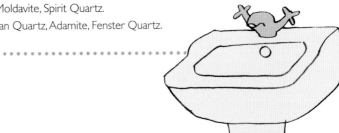

DIFFICULT TIMES

We often talk of hitting rock bottom, but in a world that's round, there's no such thing. You can feel as though you've reached the end of your tether, though, and at such times, holding on to hope is vital. Darkness can't destroy light. It can conceal it, but it can never take away its glow. The smallest of candles can brighten up the darkest of rooms. Holding a Fire Opal by your heart will light hope's flame, and help you shine through your darkest hours.

Write a list of all the bad things you've dealt with in your life, and all the obstacles you've overcome, and read through it with a Mahogany Obsidian by your heart. Solace is to be found in recognizing that you've surmounted past difficulties, and the gem will remind you that your current troubles will pass, too.

When you can find no immediate way ahead, hold a Chinese Red Quartz by your heart to help you see the flowers, rather than the weeds, in your past's garden; and when you really think that you can't go on, hold an Orange Flint over your feet to give you courage, over your third eye to heed its knowledge, and over your heart to bring you peace.

Alternative gemstones:
Fire Opal: Garnet, Atacamite, Boulder Opal.
Mahogany Obsidian: Onyx, Rhyolite, Chiastolite.
Chinese Red Quartz: Strawberry Quartz, Blue Aragonite, Ouro Verde Quartz.
Orange Flint: Boulder Opal, Celestite, Rutilated Quartz.

Unlock your inner confidence
Look at your reflection with warmth and affection by holding a Pink Aura Quartz by your heart, and blowing yourself a kiss in the mirror to encourage you to love, honor, and obey yourself—today, tomorrow, and happily ever after. **Alternative gemstones:** Pink Crackle Quartz, Pink Danburite, Yellow Spinel.

Harness protective energy
Be moved by the world without being broken by it—like a tree swaying in the wind by sitting with your back against a tree while holding a Magnetite to prevent other people's sorrow from leaving you feeling empty. **Alternative gemstones:** Kunzite, Ruby, Aventurine.

Rediscovering enthusiasm
When you look at a dandelion, what do you see—a wish to be granted or an annoying weed? Reawaken your childhood zest for life by holding a Youngite by your heart, or wearing one around your neck. **Alternative gemstones:** Pink Sunstone, Alexandrite, Ajoite.

Expressing yourself
Many of us hide our true selves from the world, never knowing who could be longing to meet the person we've locked away. Do them, and yourself, justice by wearing a Sunstone necklace to empower you to reveal your inner beauty to others. **Alternative gemstones:** Variscite, Howlite, Jade.

Embrace your kookiness
The philosopher Nietzsche once said, "Those who danced were thought to be quite mad by those who couldn't hear the music." Be your own kind of kooky fabulous by hanging a Zoisite on your brightest necklace to lessen your fear of ridicule. **Alternative gemstones:** Aegrine, Blue Lace Agate, Charoite.

ALEXANDRITE

Forgiving yourself
They say forgiveness is a virtue, and no one deserves it more than you do. Spend five minutes wishing to be happy, healthy, and free from suffering each evening while holding an Infinite Stone by your heart. Sleep with the gem under your pillow, knowing those wishes will soon come true. **Alternative gemstones:** Tugtupite, Eudialyte, Ajoite.

HOWLITE

Let go of your past mistakes
If the past were human, it would have been arrested, charged, and locked up long ago, because it's definitely the guiltiest thief of all. It robs us of the joy of today. Keep a Heulandite by your bedside clock to inspire you to move forward, like the clock's hands, and forgive your past woes. **Alternative gemstones:** Hematite, Snowflake Obsidian, Muscovite.

ZOISITE

Freedom from self-limiting beliefs
You have a treasure of wealth inside you, and when you start believing in yourself, others will believe in you, too. Place a list of your proudest achievements in a pouch with an Astrophyllite and hold it near your heart to turn your limiting beliefs into limitless ones. **Alternative gemstones:** Strawberry Quartz, Pink Petalite, Unakite.

MUSCOVITE

UNAKITE

AJOITE

Leaving the past behind
Swap living in the past for having a blast by writing a list of everything holding you back and tying it to a balloon. Hold a Cinnabar Jasper, take your balloon outside, and let it go so it's free like a dragonfly. Your broken wings will open again soon.
Alternative gemstones: Danburite, Manganoan Calcite, Vivianite.

Self-created guilt
The next time you're feeling guilty about something, write it on a piece of glass with a felt-tipped pen, hold a Voegesite by your heart, and throw your confession into the ocean or a lake. Watch as your sorrow disappears into the water, leaving you and your conscience guilt-free. **Alternative gemstones:** Chrysocolla, Eudialyte, Cobaltoan Calcite.

Personal growth
Growing older might be inevitable, but growing up is definitely optional! Make sure your inner and outer world stay in sync by starting a diary. Every evening, hold a Boulder Opal and jot down everything you've learned that day to help you become wiser with age. **Alternative gemstones:** Tourmaline, Amazonite, Aquamarine.

BORNITE

Be happy
According to an old African proverb, "When there is no enemy within, the enemies outside cannot hurt you." Wear a Clear Phenacite necklace to ensure you beautify, rather than tarnish, your soul with the seeds you sow in its garden. **Alternative gemstones:** Apophyllite, Bornite, Idocrase.

Humor
A laugh a day keeps the blues away. Affirm this to yourself whenever life gets too serious. Look in a mirror, hold a Pyromorphite on your forehead, and pull the silliest face you can. You'll soon feel chirpier.
Alternative gemstones: Goethite, Watermelon Tourmaline, Pink Crackle Quartz.

Crystal Fact
Quartz crystal is said to make you less cynical.

Achieve inner harmony
Give your mind a rest by placing a Dalmatian Stone on your forehead any time you start feeling exhausted by your thoughts. Imagine the gem absorbing all of your tension, and filling your body with its calming vibration. Then close your eyes and smile.
Alternative gemstones: Ametrine, Halite, White Calcite.

Staying positive Place a Tangerine Quartz by your heart any time your hope waivers to help you see the good in every goodbye, the ray of sunshine in every betrayal, and the trophy in every catastrophe. **Alternative gemstones:** Anhydrite, Azeztulite, Stibnite.

Sharing hope As Buddha said, "Thousands of candles can be lit from a single candle and the life of the candle will not be shortened." Happiness never decreases by being shared, and hope is the same. Send a Calcite to someone who's lost their hope to relight it with yours. **Alternative gemstones:** Mangano Calcite, Lepidocrite, Blue Quartz.

SILVER

Staying strong Hope is the little voice telling you to "keep trying" when your faith is waning. Wear a Variscite to strengthen your belief in brighter tomorrows, and to help you stay strong till the end of your troubles. **Alternative gemstones:** Moss Agate, Pietersite, Spectrolite.

Removing blocks to healing As writer Haruki Murakami once said, "Pain is inevitable. Suffering is optional." Hold an Okenite by your heart, or wear one around your neck, to ensure you're the healer of your sadness, rather than the one encouraging it to linger. **Alternative gemstones:** Morganite, Mangano Calcite, Blue Obsidian.

Silence your inner critic There's a bad wolf inside us all—a horrible creature, always waiting for that one chance to spoil our soul's rapture. Hold a Scapolite by your heart to silence the voice of your beast, knowing you and your mind will soon be left in peace. **Alternative gemstones:** Black Actinolite, Tourmalinated Quartz, Larimar.

Be at peace with yourself Find inner peace by viewing yourself as a masterpiece—no one can see the mistakes except the artist. Spend an evening painting with your eyes closed while holding an Actinollite Quartz to help you see how coloring outside the lines can still create something truly sublime. **Alternative gemstones:** Variscite, Beryllonite, Diopside.

The power of imagination A life without imagination is like a world without birdsong—still beautiful, but not quite as wonderful. Place an Ulexite under your pillow to keep yours strong. Then wherever you are, and whatever you're going through, your life will always be full of song. **Alternative gemstones:** Diamond, Rose Quartz, Opal.

Unlock hidden talents

Keep an Andratite Garnet on your desk to help you turn your emotional bruises into artistic form, and unlock the talent within. **Alternative gemstones:** Amber, Ametrine, Apatite.

Following your intuition

Turn your inner knowledge into a source of courage by holding a Vivianite on your third eye to incite your intuition to awaken, and help you find the salvation you seek within. **Alternative gemstones:** Rutile, Tiffany Stone, Annabergite.

Seeing your true self

"I am" are two of the most powerful words in the world. Make sure you know what goes after them by meditating with an Orange Phantom Quartz. Don't leave the world thinking, "Darn, I wish I'd got to know that person better." **Alternative gemstones:** Obsidian, Lilac Quartz, Silver.

Authenticity

"In order to be irreplaceable one must always be different." Channel Coco Chanel's wisdom by wearing an Indicolite to inspire you to be your own kind of beautiful, and the best and most authentic you possible. **Alternative gemstones:** Goshenite, Bronzite, Turquoise.

Individuality

Oprah Winfrey was once told to change her name to Susie to appeal to more people. She didn't, and went on to become America's first African-American billionaire. Wear an Aegrine to help you see your uniqueness as a blessing rather than weakness. **Alternative gemstones:** Diamond, Topaz, Sugilite.

Self-destructive thoughts

Confidence, like a forest, can take years to flourish, but only moments to destroy. Hold a Sichuan Quartz by your heart to obliterate the flames of your inner critic, and ensure you aren't the one lighting the match. **Alternative gemstones:** Black Actinolite, Agrellite, Turquoise.

Self-judgment

Judgment loves company and rarely comes to us alone. We judge others for not living up to our expectations, then judge ourselves for misjudging them. Place an Ajoite by your heart to help you forgive your past errors. **Alternative gemstones:** Snowflake Obsidian, Eudialyte, Sunstone.

Crystal Fact

Diamonds are believed to improve eyesight.

Crystal Fact

Turquoise is believed to prevent travel sickness.

ANHYDRITE

RUTILE

OVERCOMING INJUSTICE

FIRE OPAL

There was once a Welsh goddess, Rhiannon, who was falsely accused of murdering her son, and punished by her kingdom. She accepted her fate with dignity, and was eventually exonerated and reunited with her child, who had been kidnapped. Feeling anger at injustice is natural, so accepting the situation is not easy. A Citrine Spirit Quartz by your heart or around your neck will prevent your anger from harming you further, while a Fire Opal, symbolizing Rhiannon's virtuous qualities, will help you to forgive those who have wronged you, as she did.

BOJI STONE

If you need to take more action to help you deal with your sense of unfairness, write the word injustice down the edge of a page and then one thing you've learned from the experience next to each letter. Make it rhyme if you can, and read through it with a Boji Stone by your heart to help you see the blessings in your heartache.

PREHNITE

Otherwise, place a Lemon Chrysoprase in a musical jewelry box, and spend five minutes each night watching the ballerina dancing around to remind you that what goes around comes around, and that in time karma will prevail.

SEPTARIAN

Alternative gemstones:

Citrine Spirit Quartz: Tugtupite, Peach Selenite, Chrysoberyl.
Fire Opal: Prehnite, Sugilite, Chrysoberyl.
Boji Stone: Fire Opal, Watermelon Tourmaline, Actinolite Quartz.
Lemon Chrysoprase: Rhodonite, Limonite, Variscite.

VARISCITE

Song of yourself

There is nothing more unjust than keeping your inner music hushed. Make sure your song lives on by recording your life in a journal. Hold a Septarian while writing the entries each night, knowing that your story deserves to be told, and is more precious than any piece of gold. **Alternative gemstones:** Orange Phantom Quartz, Diamond, Yellow Topaz.

ACTINOLITE QUARTZ

Crystal Fact

The name "Rhodonite" comes from the Greek word "rhodos," meaning rose.

WATERMELON TOURMALINE

THE POWER CRYSTAL: CARNELIAN

Astrological sign: Leo

Planet: Sun

Element: Fire

Chakras: Sacral, Base

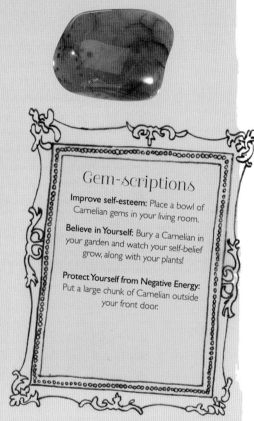

A gorgeous, "feel-better" stone, **Carnelian** is an orange variety of chalcedony that has been prized since ancient times for its ability to bestow courage, energy, and eloquence upon its owner.

Carnelian will give you the courage and self-belief to overcome difficulties and defend what you believe in. It will soothe your soul and promote a sense of idealism. If your spirits are low and you feel lethargic, let high-energy **Carnelian** restore your vitality and motivation.

This captivating gem will give you the self-belief needed to embrace change, live your dreams, and achieve your highest goals. **Carnelian** can also be used to enhance your spiritual energy, allowing you to awaken to your true talents and appreciate the beauty around you. The powerful energy of this fiery stone will revitalize and invigorate mind, body, and spirit.

Known as the "artist's stone," **Carnelian** has been associated with the fiery colors of the rising sun for centuries, and encourages us to shine our light brightly, and share our gifts with the world.

Gem-scriptions

Improve self-esteem: Place a bowl of Carnelian gems in your living room.

Believe in Yourself: Bury a Carnelian in your garden and watch your self-belief grow, along with your plants!

Protect Yourself from Negative Energy: Put a large chunk of Carnelian outside your front door.

spiritual cocktails ... enhance your self-worth

Carnelian + Bronzite = learn to love yourself and your unique qualities

Carnelian + Peridot = enhance your natural charisma

Carnelian + Blue Kyanite = tap into your creativity and discover hidden talents

INNER VOICE

As children, we're taught mathematics, science, and foreign languages but we are never told how to interpret the words in our hearts. We have to teach ourselves to trust our own judgment. Holding a Porphyrite will inspire you to listen to your inner voice. You're the only one who can understand its vocabulary and, once you're on good speaking terms, you should listen to its advice, because your inner voice is the friend you should trust most. Meditating with a Quartz on Sphalerite by your heart will help.

The truth is that we're all much smarter than we think we are, stronger than we believe, and capable of more than we think possible. Any time you're seeking answers, meditate with an Aragonite beside you and your inner voice will bring you the solutions. If you need more help, carry a Chevron Amethyst with you wherever you go and sleep with it under your pillow. Each evening, hold the crystal and focus on the problem for five minutes and your answer will come to you.

Alternative gemstones:
Porphyrite: Amazonite, Magnetite, Tiger's Eye.
Quartz on Sphalerite: Selenite, Quartz with Mica, Bustamite with Sugilite.
Aragonite: White Calcite, Phantom Quartz, Rhyolite.
Chevron Amethyst: Pink-Banded Agate, Chlorite, Rhyolite.

Crystal Fact

Moonstone is thought to balance your sex drive.

Make peace with growing older
We often speak of youth being wasted on the young, but wisdom in our older years can be wasted on us, too. Hold an Eclipse Stone to prevent your sadness about no longer being young from stopping you cherishing who you've become. **Alternative gemstones:** Moonstone, Cleavelandite, Chrysoprase.

Deepening your meditation practice
Place a Wonder Stone beside you when you're meditating to calm and quieten your mind, and help you sink into the depths of your inner world—like a pebble thrown into a river—and discover your soul's treasure. **Alternative gemstones:** Tanzanite, Elbaite, Moonstone.

Past blocks
Sometimes our past impacts on our future and prevents us from trying new experiences. Hold a Tinguaite by your heart to prevent the symptoms of your past from enduring, and to help you move on. **Alternative gemstones:** Danburite, Pink Petalite, Rhodonite.

Overcome past disappointments
A little girl once asked her mother why all parents let their children believe in Santa, only to tell them the truth when they are a bit older. Her mother told her that this small disappointment helped to prepare children for the bigger ones that life would bring! Hold a Lavender-Pink Smithsonite to help you see the strength you've gained from your previous disappointments. **Alternative gemstones:** Lepidocrosite, Sunstone, Oregon Opal.

DANBURITE

SUNSTONE

Positive self-analysis
It's often not what others say about us we fear most, but what we say to ourselves. It's our own critique that we're most afraid of. Hold a Purple Scapolite by your heart to help you benefit from your self-scrutiny, and turn your inner bully into a friend. **Alternative gemstones:** Peach Aventurine, Mohawkite, Yellow Apatite.

YELLOW APATITE

Weathering the storm
Nothing comes to us without a solution—locks come with keys, lights with switches, and gems with properties to enrich us. And our experiences are the same. Wear a Kakortokite to help you accept life's stormier periods, knowing they're happening for a reason. **Alternative gemstones:** Garnet, Celestobarite, Fire Agate.

FIRE AGATE

Open your mind
Perception is everything. A door can keep people out, shut you inside, or let people in. Place a Chrysotile in Serpentine beside a jewelry box with its lid open to inspire you to keep the doors to your own treasure chest—your mind—fully open. **Alternative gemstones:** Coprolite, Cumberlandite, Cinnabar Jasper.

VIVIANITE

Don't be in denial
Buddha was a prince who had been protected from the world's suffering. One day he ventured into the streets and was shocked to discover that everyone, including him, would die. Hold a Vivianite to prevent you from closing your mind to the truths you are trying to ignore. **Alternative gemstones:** Porphorite, Rhodochrosite, Morganite.

CHLORITE

AJOITE

Changing your story

The stories we tell ourselves are like a spider's web—we latch on to something and then keep going over and over it until we can't even see where it started from. Wear a Spider Web Obsidian to help you see through the webs of deceit you have woven in your mind. **Alternative gemstones:** Magnesite, Oregon Opal, Unakite.

Staying optimistic

We all love holidays, but why save all that happiness for just one day or one week when you can have it every day? Wear a Pyrope Garnet by your heart to inspire you to give like it's Christmas, love like it's Valentine's Day, and celebrate like it's your birthday every day. **Alternative gemstones:** Pink Crackle Quartz, Pink Chalcedony, Ruby.

Be patient with yourself

The only person you ever need to be better than is the one you were at your lowest. True success is about progress. It isn't about being the best, or better than the rest, but doing your best. Hold a Peridot to help you remember that. **Alternative gemstones:** Rhodochrosite, Mangano Calcite, Tiger's Eye.

Predicting the future

Seeking an insight into what the future has in store? Pop a few gems in a pouch and pick three randomly. Here are some of their meanings:

Sardonyx: a wedding.
Turquoise: travel.
Ruby: good fortune.
Agate: a pleasant surprise.
Garnet: a letter's on the way.
Diamond: business advancement.
Hematite: new opportunities.

HEMATITE POLISHED AND HEMATITE IN ITS NATURAL STATE.

Crystal guidance

Sometimes we know what needs to be done, but need it to be crystal clear before we are able to move forward. Spread a few gems on the floor, close your eyes, pick one, and follow its guidance:

Amethyst: a life change.
Rose Quartz: healing is needed.
Topaz: exercise caution.
Opal: an ending.
Snowflake Obsidian: end of troubles.
Clear Quartz: permanence.
Unakite: compromise.

TOPAZ

Persevering through challenges
Muhammad Ali once said, "I hated every minute of training, but I said to myself, 'Do this now, and you'll be a champion forever.'" And he went on to become the world's greatest boxer. Hold a Preseli Bluestone to help you turn what could break you into the making of you. **Alternative gemstones:** Jasper, Indian Granite, Fire Agate.

Staying true to yourself
Everyone has an opinion on everything and it's easy to be influenced by other people. Hold a Macedonian Green Opal to ensure you follow your own wisdom. **Alternative gemstones:** Diamond, Tanzanite, Sunstone.

Don't give up on your dream
When you regret not doing or saying something, it's like saying it can't happen. But there's always a chance to heal your heart's sorrow—we call it tomorrow. Write down your regret while holding a Hematite Included Quartz to remind you the dreams of your past are still within your grasp. **Alternative gemstones:** Chrysanthemum Stone, Citrine, Diamond.

Crystal Fact

Hematite boosts your chances of a payrise. Place one on your desk in the days before your annual review at work.

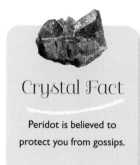
Be realistic Willow trees are thought to have originally stood upright, but were so saddened by the world's plight, they bent over in sadness, vowing to stand straight only when happiness came to all. Wear a Scapolite to prevent you from punishing yourself for what couldn't be helped. **Alternative gemstones:** Agrellite, Larimar, Tourmalinated Quartz.

Lovely attributes Some gems were traveling from the earth to the sun, and collected all of the colors of a rainbow on their way, thus creating Tourmaline. Wear one to help you appreciate the beautiful traits you've picked up on your travels, too. **Alternative gemstones:** Goethite, Chrysoprase, Rose Quartz.

Self-esteem My favorite quote of all time comes from Oprah Winfrey: "I was once afraid of people saying, 'Who does she think she is?' Now I have the courage to stand and say, 'This is who I am.' " Repeat these words to yourself each and every day, with a Sunstone, until you feel exactly the same way. **Alternative gemstones:** Lazulite, Pumice, Strawberry Quartz.

Positive self-image When we look for gems, we don't go for the lightest or brightest; we value the qualities within. Wear an Azotic Topaz to help you walk into any room as if there's a crown on your head, hot lover waiting in bed, and rose petals everywhere you tread! **Alternative gemstones:** Pearl Spa Dolomite, Pink Crackle Quartz, Candle Quartz.

Be kind to yourself

"Forgiveness is the fragrance the violet sheds on the heel that crushed it." Mark Twain was right. According to myth, these flowers were created when the goddess Diana protected a nymph by turning her into a violet. Hold an Iolite, derived from "ios," meaning violet, to heal any self-blame. **Alternative gemstones:** Brandenberg, Rutilated Quartz, Peridot.

Shake off an inferiority complex No matter how small you feel on the inside, no one can see that on the outside. We all come in different shapes and sizes physically, but our hearts have the same capacity. Hold a Yellow Jasper to help you realize that feeling inferior is just a mindset that can be changed. **Alternative gemstones:** Pink Sapphire, Lavender-Pink Smithsonite, Garnet.

Believe in yourself To achieve anything, you need to believe in yourself. Place a plant in your garden with a Stichtite in the pot, to help you sow the seeds of your self-belief, knowing that you will reap happiness. **Alternative gemstones:** Magnetite, Carnelian, Calcite.

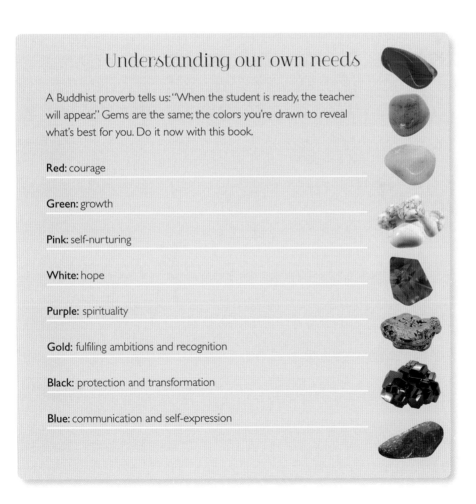

Understanding our own needs

A Buddhist proverb tells us: "When the student is ready, the teacher will appear." Gems are the same; the colors you're drawn to reveal what's best for you. Do it now with this book.

Red: courage

Green: growth

Pink: self-nurturing

White: hope

Purple: spirituality

Gold: fulfiling ambitions and recognition

Black: protection and transformation

Blue: communication and self-expression

Accepting uncertainty The sea never knows what's in store; it relies entirely on the planet, sun, and moon to control its movement. Place a Star Hollandite Quartz beside a picture of the ocean to help you embrace the uncertainty of life's motion. **Alternative gemstones:** Apophyllite, Anhydrite, Larimar.

Be imaginative Ancient Persians used to believe the world was seated on a giant Blue Sapphire, which painted the sky blue, and reflected the color of heaven. Wear one to inspire you to see the world as colorfully as they did. **Alternative gemstones:** Cavansite, Nebula Stone, Eilat Stone.

Have a zest for life "Sing like no one is listening, love like you've never been hurt, dance like nobody is watching, and live like it's heaven on earth." Write Mark Twain's beautiful words on a piece of card, and keep it in your home by a Pink Chalcedony to ensure you do all the above—and more! **Alternative gemstones:** Pink Crackle Quartz, Strawberry Quartz, Morganite.

X-factor for all occasions

Need to wow right now? Here's how. Simply keep a range of different colored gems in your bag, and pick the hue that's right for the way you're feeling. Try it now.

Orange: confidence and self-esteem

White: originality and inspiration

Yellow: logic and memory

Green: beauty and wellbeing

Brown: practicality and learning

Silver: good luck and intuition

NURTURE YOUR CREATIVITY

Singing and dancing, writing, painting—who hasn't wished to be good at one or other of these at some time in their lives? If any or all are a challenge, that's no reason not to try. You can get your creative juices flowing by placing an Orange Calcite crystal under your pillow to stimulate your imagination, and ensure you wake up feeling really motivated, and ready for some serious artistic action.

Give yourself a Ginger Rogers-style makeover by wearing a Carnelian necklace to boost your performing mojo. It's a great crystal for dancers and actors, and will give your karaoke performances a show-stopping edge, too! However, if you were born with the singing skills of a vocally-challenged parrot, you may need to harness your inner disco diva by playing your favorite song and holding a Kyanite by your throat to improve your musical abilities, and to help you sing like an angel.

If you long to be a wordsmith, awaken your inner Shakespeare by placing a piece of Turquoise beside your laptop or writing journal to unlock your writing talents, and help you weave words together perfectly. And an absolute must for would-be artists is Picasso Marble. Place one in your work room to help you see and capture all the beauty around you, and inspire you to share your gift with the world.

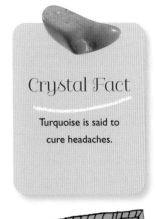

Crystal Fact

Turquoise is said to cure headaches.

Alternative gemstones:
Orange Calcite: Fire Agate, Labradorite, Tourmaline.
Carnelian: Blue Kyanite, Blue Calcite, Thulite.
Kyanite: Rhodochrosite, Rhodonite, Apatite.
Turquoise: Citrine, Dolomite, Rose Quartz.
Picasso Marble: Celestite, Ametrine, Tiger Iron.

BLUE CALCITE

Conclusion

So dear reader, here we are at the end of our journey together. But before I leave you till we meet again, I'd like to tell you about how my truly amazing and life-changing journey with this book ended.

In the weeks following its completion, I found myself feeling a little lost; the book had been such a huge and wonderful part of my life for so long, I felt lonely without it. So one night I said a little prayer to my crystals (as I do every night), and asked them to give me a sign. The next day I walked into town, and saw a beautiful crystal stall with the words "happy stones" written across the top; it was the first time its owners—two worldly gem traders from Brazil—had ever sold their gems in this country.

Enchanted, I returned to the stall every day for the next week, captivated by the gems I'd loved, researched, and written about for years—but in some cases never actually seen until that moment.

One day as I was admiring the gems for the umpteenth time, one of the traders, deeply touched by my genuine love and passion for the crystals, gave me one—just like the little girl in my past-life regression. I now keep it under my pillow every night—like she did—to remind me that my journey, like yours, has really only just begun.

So my wonderful and brave friend, I hope the rituals and crystals in this book, as well as my personal story, have inspired you to see the rose quartzes in every garden, gold in both your own and other people's hearts, and silver lining to every cloud, so you can look in the mirror, and wholeheartedly love, appreciate, and marvel at what you see.

I also hope you'll write to tell me about your wonderful crystal experiences. I'd love to read your crystal stories so please do email me at to_gol@hotmail.com, find me on Facebook (Naz Says), or follow me on Instagram (@naz_alibagi), where you can read more of my crystal tips and follow my crystal adventures.

And just in case you need further proof of how magically powerful crystals can be, here's another little anecdote to strengthen your faith further.

When I was about 13, I used to go into a wonderful spiritual shop every day after school. My parents didn't have much money at the time, so I couldn't afford to buy anything; but each day without fail I'd go into my little magical sanctuary, and admire all the beautiful gemstones.

One day, when no one was looking, I held one by my heart and wished I'd get a book published by the time I was 30 and a diamond necklace from Tiffany & Co. at some point in my life. My book went to print two weeks before my 30th birthday. And my gift? A diamond necklace from Tiffany & Co.

Stockists

Best Crystals
www.bestcrystals.com

Charms of Light
www.charmsoflight.com

Coleman's Crystal Mines and
Rock Shop
www.jimcolemancrystals.com

Crystals and Jewelry
www.crystalsandjewelry.com

The Crystal Garden
www.thecrystalgarden.com

The Crystal Healer
www.thecrystalhealer.co.uk

The Crystal Room
www.crystalsmtshasta.com

Crystal Vaults
www.crystalvaults.com

Earth Gallery
www.earthgallery.com

Emily Gems
www.crystal-cure.com

Exquisite Crystals
www.exquisitecrystals.com

Healing Crystals
www.healingcrystals.com

Mineral Miners
www.mineralminers.com

Peaceful Mind
www.peacefulmind.com

Resources

Denise Whichello Brown, *The Power of Crystals* (Bookmart, 2002)

Cassandra Eason, *Crystals for Passion and Romance* (Seven Oaks, 2014)

Cassandra Eason, *The New Crystal Bible* (Carlton Books, 2010)

Mary Lambert, *Crystal Energy* (CICO Books, 2010)

Michael Gienger, *Purifying Crystals* (Findhorn, 2008)

Michael Gienger, *Crystal Power, Crystal Healing* (Cassell, 2002)

Judy Hall, *The Crystal Bible* (Godsfield, 2013)

Judy Hall, *The Encyclopedia of Crystals* (Godsfield, 2013)

Judy Hall, *101 Power Crystals* (Fair Winds Press, 2011)

Judy Hall, *Crystal Prosperity* (Ivy Press, 2010)

Judy Hall, *Crystal Love* (Godsfield, 2008)

Simon and Sue Lilly, *The Essential Crystal Handbook* (Duncan Baird, 2006)

Simon Lilly, *Crystal Healing* (Element, 2002)

Philip Permutt, *The Complete Guide to Crystal Chakra Healing* (CICO Books, 2009)

Philip Permutt, *The Crystal Healer* (CICO Books, 2007)

Doreen Virtue & Judith Lukomski, *Crystal Therapy* (Hay House, 2005)

A–Z of Crystals

A

Abalone Shell
Star Signs: Cancer, Scorpio,
Chakra: Throat

Actinollite Quartz
Star Sign: Scorpio
Chakra: Heart

Adamite
Star Sign: Cancer
Chakra: Heart

Aegirine
Star Sign: Taurus
Chakra: Higher Heart

Afghanite
Star Sign: Aries, Virgo
Chakra: Third Eye

African Jade
Star Sign: Pisces
Chakra: Heart

Agate
Star Sign: Gemini
Chakra: See specific agates

Agrellite
Star Sign: Aquarius
Chakra: Third Eye

Ajo Blue Calcite
Star Signs: Cancer, Pisces
Chakra: Third Eye

Ajoite with Shattuckite
Star Signs: Sagittarius, Aquarius
Chakras: Throat, Heart

Alexandrite
Star Sign: Scorpio
Chakra: Heart

Almandine
Star Signs: Virgo, Scorpio
Chakras: Base and Heart

Almandine Garnet
Star Signs: Virgo, Scorpio
Chakras: Base, Sacral, Heart

Amazonite
Star Sign: Virgo
Chakra: Heart

Amber
Star Signs: Leo, Aquarius
Chakras: Sacral, Solar Plexus

Amblygonite
Star Sign: Taurus
Chakra: Solar Plexus

Amethyst
Star Signs: Virgo, Capricorn,
Chakra: Crown

Ametrine
Star Sign: Libra
Chakras: Solar Plexus, Crown

Ammolite
Star Sign: Aquarius
Chakras: Root, Brow

Andalusite
Star Signs: Virgo, Pisces
Chakra: All

Andradite Garnet
Star Sign: Aquarius
Chakra: Base

Angelite
Star Sign: Aquarius
Chakra: Throat

Angel Aura Quartz
Star Signs: All
Chakra: All

Anhydrite
Star Signs: Cancer, Scorpio
Chakras: Sacral, Solar Plexus

Anthrophyllite
Star Sign: Virgo
Chakra: Base

Annabergite
Star Sign: Capricorn
Chakra: Base

Apache Tear
Star Sign: Aries
Chakra: Base

Apatite
Star Sign: Gemini
Chakra: Throat

Apophyllite
Star Signs: Gemini, Libra
Chakras: Brow, Crown

Aqua Aura
Star Sign: Leo
Chakras: Brow, Throat

Aquamarine
Star Signs: Aries, Gemini, Pisces
Chakra: Throat

Aragonite
Star Sign: Capricorn
Chakra: Crown

Arfvedsonite
Star Sign: Gemini
Chakra: Crown

Astrophyllite
Star Signs: Virgo, Scorpio, Aries
Chakra: Crown

Atacamite
Star Sign: Aquarius
Chakras: Heart, Brow

Atlantasite
Star Signs: Virgo, Libra
Chakra: Brow

Aurichalcite
Star Sign: Aquarius
Chakra: None

Avalonite
Star Signs: Cancer, Sagittarius
Chakras: Heart, Sacral

Aventurine
Star Sign: Aries
Chakra: Heart

Azeztulite
Star Signs: All
Chakra: All

Azotic Topaz
Star Sign: Sagittarius
Chakra: Solar Plexus

Azurite
Star Sign: Sagittarius
Chakra: Throat

B

Barite
Star Sign: Aquarius
Chakra: Throat

Basalt
Star Sign: None
Chakra: None

Bastnasite
Star Signs: Scorpio, Capricorn
Chakra: Base

Benitoite
Star Sign: None
Chakra: All

Beryl
Star Signs: Aries, Gemini, Leo,
Chakras: Crown, Solar Plexus

Beryllonite
Star Sign: Aries
Chakra: Crown

Black Actinolite
Star Sign: Scorpio
Chakra: Root

Black Agate
Star Sign: Capricorn
Chakra: Base

Black Moonstone
Star Sign: Cancer
Chakra: Sacral

Black Obsidian
Star Sign: Sagittarius
Chakra: Base

Black Opal
Star Signs: Cancer, Scorpio
Chakra: Base

Black Onyx
Star Sign: Leo
Chakra: Base

Black Sapphire
Star Signs: Virgo, Sagittarius
Chakra: Brow

Black Tourmaline
Star Sign: Capricorn
Chakra: Base

Blood of Isis
Star Signs: Cancer, Leo
Chakra: Base

Bloodstone
Star Signs: Aries, Libra, Pisces
Chakra: Heart

Blue Agate
Star Signs: Pisces, Gemini
Chakras: Throat, Brow

Blue Aragonite
Star Sign: Capricorn
Chakra: Crown

Blue Calcite
Star Sign: Cancer
Chakra: Throat

Blue Chalcedony
Star Sign: Cancer, Sagittarius
Chakra: Throat

Blue Crackle Quartz
Star Sign: None
Chakra: None

Blue Drusy Quartz
Star Sign: Aries
Chakra: Crown

Blue Euclase
Star Sign: Virgo
Chakra: Heart

Blue-Green Smithsonite
Star Signs: Virgo, Pisces
Chakra: Heart

Blue Holly Agate
Star Sign: Virgo
Chakra: Brow

Blue Howlite
Star Sign: Gemini
Chakras: Crown, Brow

Blue Jade
Star Signs: Aries, Taurus
Chakras: Heart, Brow

Blue Kyanite
Star Signs: Aries, Taurus, Libra
Chakra: Throat

Blue Lace Agate
Star Sign: Pisces
Chakra: Throat

Blue Moonstone
Star Signs: Cancer, Libra
Chakra: Sacral

Blue Obsidian
Star Sign: Aquarius
Chakra: Brow

Blue Opal
Star Sign: Taurus, Cancer
Chakra: Throat

Blue Phantom Quartz
Star Signs: Aquarius, Sagittarius
Chakra: Heart

Blue Quartz
Star Signs: Taurus, Libra
Chakra: Throat

Blue Sapphire
Star Signs: Virgo, Libra
Chakra: Brow

Blue Scapolite
Star Sign: Taurus
Chakra: Brow

Blue Topaz
Star Signs: Sagittarius, Virgo
Chakra: Throat

Blue Tourmaline
Star Signs: Taurus, Libra
Chakra: All

Boji Stone
Star Signs: Taurus, Leo, Scorpio
Chakra: Base

Boli Stone
Star Sign: Pisces
Chakra: Crown

Bornite
Star Sign: Cancer
Chakra: All

Bornite on Silver
Star Sign: Cancer
Chakra: All

Botswana Agate
Star Signs: Taurus, Scorpio
Chakra: Crown

Boulder Opal
Star Signs: Virgo, Libra
Chakra: Throat

Bowenite
Star Sign: Aquarius
Chakra: Heart

Brazilianite
Star Sign: Capricorn
Chakra: Heart

Brandenberg Amethyst
Star Signs: Aquarius, Pisces
Chakras: Crown, Brow

Bronzite
Star Sign: Leo
Chakra: Heart

Brown Zircon
Star Sign: Sagittarius
Chakra: Base

Brown Jade
Star Sign: Taurus
Chakra: Base

Brown Tourmaline
Star Sign: Libra
Chakra: All

Bumble Bee Jasper
Star Sign: Leo
Chakras: Base, Sacral

Bustamite
Star Sign: Libra
Chakras: Base, Sacral, Heart

Bustamite with Sugilite
Star Sign: Virgo
Chakra: Crown

C

Cacoxenite
Star Sign: Sagittarius
Chakras: Crown, Brow

Calcite
Star Sign: Cancer
Chakra: All

Calcite Fairy Stone
Star Sign: Cancer
Chakra: All

Candle Quartz
Star Sign: Cancer
Chakra: Heart

Carrollite
Star Sign: Cancer
Chakra: Base

Cassiterite
Star Sign: Sagittarius
Chakra: Base

Carnelian
Star Signs: Taurus, Cancer, Leo
Chakra: Sacral

Catlinite
Star Sign: Sagittarius
Chakra: Sacral

Cat's Eye
Star Sign: Leo
Chakras: Crown, Solar Plexus

Cavansite
Star Sign: Aquarius
Chakra: Brow

Celadonite Phantom Quartz
Star Sign: None
Chakra: None

Celestite
Star Sign: Gemini
Chakra: Brow

Celestobarite
Star Sign: Libra
Chakras: Crown, Solar Plexus

Cerussite
Star Sign: Virgo
Chakra: Base

Cervanite
Star Sign: Virgo
Chakra: Crown

Chalcedony
Star Signs: Cancer, Sagittarius
Chakra: Varies with color

Charoite
Star Signs: Scorpio, Sagittarius
Chakra: Crown

Chevron Amethyst
Star Sign: Libra
Chakra: Heart

Chiastolite
Star Sign: Libra
Chakra: Sacral

Chinese Chromium Quartz
Star Sign: None
Chakra: None

Chinese Red Quartz
Star Sign: None
Chakra: None

Chlorite
Star Sign: Sagittarius
Chakra: Heart

Chohua Jasper
Star Sign: None
Chakra: Base

Chrysanthemum Stone
Star Signs: Taurus, Aquarius
Chakra: None

Chrysoberyl
Star Sign Leo:
Chakra: Sacral

Chrysocolla
Star Signs: Taurus, Gemini
Chakra: Heart

Chrysoprase
Star Sign: Libra
Chakra: Heart

Chrysopal
Star Signs: Libra, Cancer, Pisces
Chakras: Heart, Brow

Chrysotile
Star Sign: Leo
Chakra: Base

Chrysotile in Serpentine
Star Sign: Taurus
Chakras: Base, Brow

Cinnabar
Star Sign: Leo
Chakra: Base

Cinnabar Jasper
Star Sign: Leo
Chakras: Base, Sacral

Citrine
Star Signs: Aries, Gemini, Leo
Chakra: Solar Plexus

Citrine Spirit Quartz
Star Signs: Virgo, Capricorn
Chakras: Crown, Solar Plexus

Clear Calcite
Star Sign: Cancer
Chakra: All

Clear Phenacite
Star Sign: Gemini
Chakra: Crown

Clear Quartz
Star Sign: Capricorn
Chakra: Crown

Clear Topaz
Star Sign: Sagittarius
Chakra: Crown

Cleavelandite
Star Sign: Libra
Chakra: Crown

Clinohumite
Star Sign: Taurus
Chakra: All

Cobaltoan Calcite
Star Sign: Cancer
Chakras: Heart, Throat, Brow

Common Opal
Star Signs: Cancer, Libra
Chakra: Sacral

Conichalcite
Star Sign: Pisces
Chakra: Heart

Copper
Star Sign Taurus, Sagittarius:
Chakra: Sacral

Coprolite
Star Sign: None
Chakra: None

Coral
Star Sign: Pisces
Chakra: Crown

Covellite
Star Sign: Sagittarius
Chakra: Brow

Crazy Lace Agate
Star Signs: Gemini, Capricorn
Chakra: Heart

Creedite
Star Sign: Virgo
Chakras: Throat, Crown

Crocoite
Star Sign: Aries
Chakra: Sacral

Crystalline Kyanite
Star Signs: Aries, Taurus
Chakra: Throat

Cumberlandite
Star Sign: None
Chakra: None

Cuprite
Star Sign: Aquarius
Chakras: Sacral, Base

Dalmation Stone
Star Sign: Gemini
Chakra: Base

Danburite
Star Sign: Leo
Chakra: Crown

Datolite
Star Sign: Aries
Chakra: Brow

Dendritic Agate
Star Sign: Gemini
Chakra: All

Dendritic Chalcedony
Star Sign: Cancer
Chakra: All

Desert Rose
Star Sign: Taurus
Chakras: Crown, Solar Plexus

Diamond
Star Signs: Aries, Taurus, Leo
Chakra: All

Diopside
Star Sign: None
Chakra: None

Dioptase
Star Signs: Scorpio, Sagittarius
Chakra: All

Dolomite
Star Sign: Aries
Chakra: Crown

Dream Quartz
Star Sign: None
Chakra: None

Drusy Golden Healer Quartz
Star Sign: None
Chakra: None

Dumortierite
Star Sign: Leo
Chakra: Brown

Eclipse Stone
Star Sign: None
Chakra: None

Eilat Stone
Star Sign: Cancer
Chakra: Solar Plexus

Elbaite
Star Sign: Libra
Chakra: Heart

Elestial Quartz
Star Sign: None
Chakra: Crown

Emerald
Star Signs: Aries, Taurus
Chakra: Heart

Eosphorite
Star Sign: None
Chakra: None

Epidote
Star Sign: Gemini
Chakra: Brow

Epidote in Quartz
Star Sign: Gemini
Chakra: Brow

Erythrite
Star Signs: Taurus, Virgo
Chakra: Throat

Ethiopian Opal
Star Signs: Virgo, Sagittarius
Chakra: Heart

Eudialyte
Star Sign: Aries
Chakra: Heart

Faden Quartz
Star Sign: All
Chakra: All

Falcon's Eye
Star Sign: Capricorn
Chakra: Base

Fairy Quartz
Star Sign: Cancer
Chakras: Base, Solar Plexus

Fenster Quartz
Star Sign: Aquarius
Chakra: All

Fire Agate
Star Sign: Aries
Chakra: Brow

Fire Opal
Star Signs: Cancer, Leo, ;ibra
Chakras: Brow, Sacral

Fiskenaesset Ruby
Star Signs: Cancer, Leo
Chakra: Heart

Flint
Star Signs: Aries, Scorpio
Chakra: Crown

Fluorapatite
Star Sign: Gemini
Chakra: Crown

Fluorite
Star Signs: Capricorn, Pisces
Chakra: Brow

Fuchsite
Star Sign: Aquarius
Chakra: Heart

Gabbro
Star Sign: None
Chakra: None

Galena
Star Sign: Capricorn
Chakra: Base

Garnet
Star Signs: Leo, Virgo
Chakra: Heart

Gaspeite
Star Sign: None
Chakra: Heart

Goethite
Star Sign: Aries
Chakra: Brow

Gold
Star Sign: Leo
Chakra: Heart

Golden Apatite
Star Sign: Gemini
Chakra: Throat

Golden Beryl
Star Sign: Leo
Chakras: Crown, Solar Plexus

Golden Ray Calcite
Star Sign: Leo
Chakras: Crown, Solar Plexus

Golden Tiger's Eye
Star Signs: Capricorn, Leo
Chakras: Solar Plexus, Brow

Golden Topaz
Star Sign: Sagittarius
Chakra: Sacral

Goldstone
Star Sign: Gemini
Chakra: Base

Goshenite
Star Sign: Libra
Chakra: Brow

Graphic Smoky Quartz
Star Sign: Capricorn
Chakra: Base

Gray-Banded Agate
Star Sign: Scorpio
Chakra: Sacral

Green Agate
Star Sign: Virgo
Chakra: Heart

Green Aventurine
Star Sign: Aries
Chakra: Heart

Green Calcite
Star Sign: Cancer
Chakra: Heart

Green Fluorite
Star Signs: Capricorn, Pisces
Chakra: Heart

Green Garnet
Star Signs: Leo, Virgo
Chakra: Heart

Green Jade
Star Signs: Aries, Taurus
Chakra: Heart

Green Jasper
Star Sign: Leo
Chakra: Base

Green Moss Agate
Star Sign: Virgo
Chakras: Heart, Base, Throat

Green Phantom Quartz
Star Sign: Sagittarius
Chakras: Crown, Base

Green Obsidian
Star Sign: Gemini
Chakras: Heart, Throat

Green Opal
Star Signs: Aries, Cancer
Chakra: Heart

Green Opalite
Star Sign: Aries, Sagittarius
Chakra: Heart

Green Quartz
Star Sign: None
Chakra: Heart

Green Sapphire
Star Signs: Gemini, Leo
Chakras: Brow, Heart

Green Selenite
Star Sign: Taurus
Chakra: Crown

Green Spinel
Star Signs: Libra
Chakra: Heart

Green Tourmaline
Star Sign: Libra
Chakra: None

Greenlandite
Star Sign: None
Chakra: None

Grossularite
Star Sign: Cancer
Chakra: Heart

Gypsum
Star Sign: Aries
Chakra: Crown

Hackmanite
Star Sign: None
Chakra: None

Halite
Star Signs: Cancer, Pisces
Chakra: Sacral

Hawk's Eye
Star Signs: Capricorn, Leo
Chakras: Brow, Base

Heliodor
Star Sign: Leo
Chakras: Solar Plexus, Crown

Hematite
Star Signs: Aries, Aquarius
Chakra: Base

Hematite included Quartz
Star Sign: Taurus
Chakra: Base

Hematoid Calcite
Star Sign: Cancer
Chakra: Sacral

Hemimorphite
Star Sign: Libra
Chakra: Throat

Hessonite
Star Sign: Aries
Chakras: Sacral, Solar Plexus

Hessonite Garnet
Star Sign: Aries
Chakras: Solar Plexus, Base

Heulandite
Star Sign: Sagittarius
Chakra: None

Hiddenite
Star Sign: Scorpio
Chakra: Brow

Honey Calcite
Star Sign: Aries
Chakra: Sacral

Honey Opal
Star Sign: None
Chakra: None

Howlite
Star Sign: Gemini
Chakra: Crown

Ice Quartz
Star Sign: Capricorn
Chakra: Heart

Iceland Spar
Star Signs: Gemini, Cancer
Chakra: All

Icicle Calcite
Star Sign: Cancer
Chakras: Sacral, Solar Plexus

Idocrase
Star Sign: Sagittarius
Chakra: Heart

Imperial Topaz
Star Signs: Leo, Sagittarius
Chakras: Solar Plexus, Crown

Indian Granite
Star Sign: None
Chakra: None

Indicolite
Star Signs: Taurus, Libra
Chakras: Throat, Brow

Infinite Stone
Star Sign: Gemini
Chakra: All

Iolite
Star Signs: Libra, Sagittarius
Chakra: Brown

Iridescent Pyrite
Star Sign: Leo
Chakra: Solar Plexus

Iron Pyrite
Star Sign: Leo
Chakra: Solar Plexus

Jade
Star Signs: Aries, Taurus, Libra
Chakra: Heart

Jadeite
Star Sign: Aries
Chakra: Heart

Jamesonite
Star Sign: None
Chakra: None

Jasper
Star Sign: Leo
Chakra: Base

Jet
Star Sign: Capricorn
Chakra: Base

K

Kakortokite
Star Sign: None
Chakra: None

Khutnohorite
Star Sign: None
Chakra: None

Kornerupine
Star Sign: None
Chakra: None

Kunzite
Star Signs: Aries, Taurus, Leo
Chakra: Heart

Kyanite
Star Signs: Aries, Taurus, Libra
Chakra: Throat

L

Labradorite
Star Signs: Leo, Scorpio
Chakra: Crown

Lapis Lazuli
Star Sign: Sagittarius
Chakra: Brow

Larimar
Star Sign: Leo
Chakra: Heart

Larvakite
Star Signs: Leo, Scorpio
Chakra: Base

Lavender Jade
Star Sign: Libra
Chakras: Base, Brow, Crown

Lavender Pink Smithsonite
Star Signs: Virgo, Pisces
Chakra: All

Lazulite
Star Sign: Gemini
Chakra: None

Lemon Chrysoprase
Star Sign: Libra
Chakra: Heart

Lemurian Jade
Star Signs: Aries, Taurus
Chakra: Heart

Leopardskin Orbicular Jade
Star Sign: Virgo
Chakra: All

Leopardskin Jasper
Star Signs: Virgo, Libra
Chakra: All

Lepidocrite
Star Sign: Sagittarius
Chakra: All

Lepidocrocite
Star Sign: Sagittarius
Chakra: All

Lepidolite
Star Sign: Libra
Chakras: Heart, Brow

Lilac Kunzite
Star Signs: Leo, Scorpio
Chakras: Crown, Brow

Lilac Quartz
Star Sign: Aries
Chakra: All

Limonite
Star Sign: Virgo
Chakra: None

Lithium Quartz
Star Sign: None
Chakra: All

Lodestone
Star Signs: Gemini, Virgo
Chakra: Base

Lodolite Quartz
Star Sign: Gemini, Virgo
Chakra: Base

Macedonian Green Opal
Star Sign: Aquarius
Chakra: Crown

Madagascar Cloudy Quartz
Star Sign: Scorpio
Chakra: All

Magnesite
Star Sign: Aries
Chakra: Crown

Magnetite
Star Signs: Aries, Virgo
Chakra: Base

Mahogany Obsidian
Star Sign: Libra
Chakra: Base

Malachite
Star Signs: Scorpio, Capricorn
Chakra: Heart

Manganoan Calcite
Star Sign: Cancer
Chakra: Heart

Marble
Star Signs: Sagittarius, Cancer
Chakra: Sacral

Marcasite
Star Sign: Leo
Chakra: Solar Plexus

Maw Sit Sit
Star Sign: None
Chakra: None

Melanite
Star Sign: Scorpio
Chakra: Heart

Merlinite
Star Sign: Pisces
Chakra: Brow

Messina Quartz
Star Sign: None
Chakra: None

Metamorphosis Quartz
Star Sign: Scorpio
Chakra: All

Meteorite
Star Sign: All
Chakras: Crown, Base

Mohawkite
Star Sign: None
Chakra: All

Moldavite
Star Sign: All
Chakras: Brow, Heart

Molybendite
Star Sign: Scorpio
Chakra: All

Mookaite
Star Sign: Leo
Chakra: Base

Moonstone
Star Sign: Cancer, Libra
Chakra: Sacral

Morganite
Star Sign: Libra
Chakra: Heart

Morganite with Azeztulite
Star Sign: Libra
Chakra: Heart

Moss Agate
Star Sign: Virgo
Chakra: Heart

Muscovite
Star Signs: Leo, Aquarius
Chakra: Heart

N

Natural Quartz
Star Sign: All
Chakra: All

Navaho Purple Turquoise
Star Signs: Scorpio, Sagittarius
Chakra: Throat

Nebula Stone
Star Sign: Scorpio
Chakra: Heart

Nirvana Quartz
Star Sign: Capricorn
Chakra: Brow

Novaculite
Star Signs: Scorpio, Crown
Chakra: Base

Nuummite
Star Sign: Sagittarius
Chakra: All

O

Obsidian
Star Signs: Aries, Scorpio
Chakra: Base

Ocean Jasper
Star Sign: Capricorn
Chakra: Heart

Okenite
Star Signs: Virgo, Sagittarius
Chakra: Crown

Onyx
Star Sign: Leo
Chakra: Base

Opal
Star Signs: Cancer, Libra
Chakras: Throat, Heart, Crown

Orange Calcite
Star Signs: Cancer, Leo
Chakra: Sacral

Orange Flint
Star Sign: Aries, Scorpio
Chakra: Crown

Orange Grossular Garnet
Star Signs: Capricorn, Cancer
Chakras: Solar Plexus, Base

Orange Jade
Star Signs: Virgo, Aries
Chakra: All

Orange Phantom Quartz
Star Sign: All
Chakras: Heart, Solar Plexus

Orange Zircon
Star Signs: Leo, Virgo
Chakras: Base, Sacral

Orchid Calcite
Star Sign: None
Chakra: None

Oregon Opal
Star Signs: Cancer, Libra, Pisces
Chakras: Throat, Solar Plexus

Orpiment
Star Sign: Capricorn
Chakra: Solar Plexus

Ouro Verde Quartz
Star Sign: None
Chakra: None

P

Paraiba Tourmaline
Star Sign: None
Chakra: None

Pargasite
Star Sign: None
Chakra: None

Peach Aventurine
Star Sign: Aries
Chakras: Heart, Sacral

Peach Selenite
Star Sign: Taurus
Chakras: Crown, Solar Plexus

Peacock Ore
Star Sign: None
Chakra: All

Pearl
Star Signs: Gemini, Cancer
Chakra: Sacral

Pearl Spa Dolomite
Star Sign: Aries
Chakra: Crown

Pentagonite
Star Sign: None
Chakra: None

Peridot
Star Signs: Leo, Virgo, Scorpio
Chakra: Heart

Petalite
Star Sign: Leo
Chakra: Crown

Petrified Wood
Star Sign: Leo
Chakra: Base

Phantom Quartz
Star Sign: All
Chakras: Heart, Crown

Phenacite
Star Sign: Gemini
Chakras: Crown, Brow

Picasso Marble
Star Signs: Sagittarius, Cancer
Chakra: Sacral

Pietersite
Star Sign: Leo
Chakra: Brow

Pineapple Amethyst
Star Sign: None
Chakra: None

Pink Aura Quartz
Star Sign: None
Chakra: None

Pink Agate
Star Signs: Libra, Capricorn
Chakra: Heart

Pink-Banded Agate
Star Signs: Taurus, Scorpio
Chakras: Heart, Sacral

Pink Calcite
Star Sign: Capricorn
Chakra: Heart

Pink Carnelian
Star Sign: Cancer
Chakra: Base

Pink Chalcedony
Star Signs: Cancer, Sagittarius
Chakra: None

Pink Crackle Quartz
Star Signs: Taurus, Libra
Chakra: Heart

Pink Danburite
Star Sign: Leo
Chakra: Crown

Pink Halite
Star Signs: Cancer, Pisces
Chakras: Heart, Crownl

Pink Kunzite
Star Signs: Aries, Taurus, Leo
Chakra: Heart

Pink Opal
Star Sign: Cancer
Chakra: Heart

Pink Petalite
Star Sign: Pisces
Chakra: Heart

Pink Phantom Quartz
Star Sign: Taurus, Libra
Chakra: Heart

Pink Sapphire
Star Signs: Virgo, Libra
Chakra: Heart

Pink Sunstone
Star Signs: Leo, Libra
Chakras: Crown, Base, Sacral

Pink Topaz
Star Signs: Libra, Sagittarius
Chakra: Heart

Pink Tourmaline
Star Sign: Libra
Chakra: Heart

Poldervaarite
Star Sign: None
Chakra: None

Poppy Jasper
Star Sign: None
Chakras: Base, Sacral

Porphory
Star Sign: None
Chakra: None

Porphyrite
Star Sign: None
Chakra: None

Prehnite
Star Sign: Libra
Chakras: Heart, Brow

Prophecy Stone
Star Sign: None
Chakra: None

Preseli Bluestone
Star Sign: None
Chakra: None

Pumice
Star Sign: None
Chakra: None

Purple Fluorite
Star Signs: Capricorn, Pisces
Chakra: Crown

Purple Moonstone
Star Signs: Cancer, Libra
Chakra: Sacral

Purple Scapolite
Star Sign: Taurus
Chakra: Brow

Purpurite
Star Sign: Virgo
Chakra: Crown

Pyrite
Star Sign: Leo
Chakra: All

Pyrite in Quartz
Star Sign: Leo
Chakra: Solar Plexus

Pyrite with Sphalerite
Star Sign: Leo
Chakra: Solar Plexus

Pyrolusite
Star Sign: Leo
Chakra: Sacral

Pyromorphite
Star Sign: Aries, Leo
Chakra: Heart

Pyrope Garnet
Star Signs: Cancer, Leo
Chakras: Base, Crown

Pyrophylllite
Star Sign: Pisces
Chakras: Sacral, Solar Plexus

Quantum Quattro
Star Sign: None
Chakra: Heart

Quartz
Star Sign: All
Chakra: All

Quartz in Gold
Star Sign: Leo
Chakra: Heart

Quartz on Sphalerite
Star Sign: Gemini
Chakras: Solar Plexus, Base

Quartz with Mica
Star Sign: Cancer
Chakras: Brow, Crown

Que Sera
Star Sign: Cancer, Capricorn
Chakra: All

Rainbow Aqua Quartz
Star Sign: None
Chakra: None

Rainbow Aura Quartz
Star Sign: None
Chakras: Heart, Crown

Rainbow Obsidian
Star Sign: Libra
Chakra: Base

Rainbow Rhyolite
Star Sign: None
Chakra: None

Rainforest Rhyolite
Star Sign: Aquarius
Chakra: Brow

Realgar
Star Sign: None
Chakra: None

Red Black Obsidian
Star Signs: Scorpio, Capricorn
Chakra: Base

Red Brown Agate
Star Signs: Scorpio, Capricorn
Chakras: Base, Sacral

Red Calcite
Star Sign: Cancer
Chakra: Base

Red Chalcedony
Star Sign: Sagittarius
Chakra: None

Red Garnet
Star Signs: Leo, Virgo, Aquarius
Chakra: Heart

Red Jasper
Star Signs: Aries, Taurus
Chakra: Base

Red Muscovite
Star Signs: Leo, Aquarius
Chakra: Heart

Red Phantom Quartz
Star Sign: None
Chakras: Base, Sacral

Red Tourmaline
Star Signs: Scorpio, Sagittarius
Chakras: Base, Sacral

Rhodochrosite
Star Signs: Leo, Scorpio
Chakra: Heart

Rhodonite
Star Sign: Taurus
Chakra: Heart

Rhodozite
Star Sign: None
Chakra: All

Rhomboid Calcite
Star Sign: Cancer
Chakra: Brow

Rhyolite
Star Sign: Sagittarius
Chakra: Base

Richterite
Star Sign: None
Chakra: Throat

Rose Aura Quartz
Star Sign: None
Chakras: Heart, Brow, Sacral

Rose Elestial Quartz
Star Sign: None
Chakra: None

Rose Quartz
Star Signs: Taurus, Libra
Chakra: Heart

Roselite
Star Sign: None
Chakra: None

Royal Plume Jasper
Star Sign: None
Chakra: Crown

Ruby
Star Signs: Cancer, Leo
Chakra: Heart

Rutilated Kunzite
Star Sign: None
Chakra: None

Rutilated Quartz
Star Sign: All
Chakras: Brow, Crown

Rutilated Topaz
Star Sign: None
Chakra: None

Rutile
Star Signs: Taurus, Gemini
Chakra: Brow

Sacred Scribe Quartz
Star Sign: None
Chakra: None

Sandstone
Star Sign: Gemini
Chakra: Sacral

Sapphire
Star Signs: Virgo, Libra
Chakra: Brow

Sardonyx
Star Sign: Aries
Chakra: Sacral

Scapolite
Star Sign: Taurus
Chakra: Brow

Schalenblende
Star Signs: Aquarius, Pisces
Chakra: Solar Plexus

Schorl
Star Sign: Capricorn
Chakra: Base

Scolectite
Star Sign: Capricorn
Chakra: Crown

Selenite
Star Sign: Taurus
Chakra: Crown

Septarian
Star Sign: Taurus
Chakra: Base

Seraphinite
Star Signs: Sagittarius
Chakras: Heart, Brow, Crownl

Serpentine
Star Sign: Gemini
Chakra: Heart

Serpentine in Obsidian
Star Sign: Gemini
Chakra: Heart

Shattuckite
Star Signs: Sagittarius, Aquarius
Chakras: Throat, Brow

Shaman Quartz
Star Sign: None
Chakra: None

Shell Jasper
Star Sign: Libra
Chakra: All

Shift Crystal Quartz
Star Sign: All
Chakra: All

Shift Quartz
Star Sign: None
Chakra: None

Shiva Lingham
Star Sign: Scorpio
Chakra: All

Siberian Green Quartz
Star Sign: None
Chakra: Heart

Sichuan Quartz
Star Sign: Virgo
Chakra: All

Sillimanite
Star Sign: Aries
Chakra: All

Silver
Star Signs: Cancer, Aquarius
Chakras: Heart, Throat, Brow

Sliver-Leaf Jasper
Star Sign: None
Chakra: None

Smithsonite
Star Signs: Virgo, Pisces
Chakra: Heart

Smoky Amethyst
Star Sign: None
Chakra: None

Smoky Cathedral Quartz
Star Sign: None
Chakra: None

Smoky Elestial
Star Signs: Scorpio, Sagittarius
Chakra: Crown

Smoky Quartz
Star Sign: Sagittarius
Chakra:: Base

Smoky Rose Quartz
Star Signs: Scorpio, Capricorn
Chakra: Base

Snakeskin Agate
Star Sign: Gemini
Chakras: Base, Sacral

Snakeskin Pyrite
Star Sign: None
Chakra: None

Snow Quartz
Star Sign: Capricorn
Chakra: Crown

Snowflake Obsidian
Star Sign: Virgo
Chakra: Base

Sodalite
Star Sign: Sagittarius
Chakra: Brow

Spectrolite
Star Signs: Leo, Scorpio
Chakra: None

Spessartine
Star Sign: Aquarius
Chakra: Sacral

Sphene
Star Sign: Sagittarius
Chakra: All

Spider Web Obsidian
Star Sign: None
Chakra: None

Spinel
Star Signs: Aries, Sagittarius
Chakra: Base

Spiral Green
Star Sign: None
Chakra: None

Spirit Quartz
Star Signs: Virgo, Capricorn
Chakra: Crown

Star Hollandite Quartz
Star Sign: None
Chakra: None

Star Sapphire
Star Sign: Sagittarius
Chakras: Throat, Brow

Staurolite
Star Sign: Pisces
Chakra: Base

Steatite
Star Sign: None
Chakra: None

Stibnite
Star Signs: Scorpio, Capricorn
Chakra: Crown

Stichtite
Star Sign: None
Chakra: None

Stone of Dreams
Star Sign: None
Chakra: None

Stone of Solidarity
Star Sign: None
Chakra: None

Strawberry Quartz
Star Sign: Libra
Chakras: Crown, Heart

Stromatolite
Star Signs: Sagittarius
Chakra: Base

Sugilite
Star Sign: Virgo
Chakra: Crown

Sulphur
Star Sign: Leo
Chakra: Solar Plexus

Sunstone
Star Sign: Leo, Libra
Chakra: Crown

Super 7
Star Sign: All
Chakra: All

T

Tangerine Quartz
Star Sign: None
Chakras: Base, Sacral

Tangerose Quartz
Star Sign: None
Chakra: None

Tanzine Aura Quartz
Star Sign: Gemini
Chakras: Throat, Crown

Tanzanite
Star Signs: Gemini, Libra
Chakras: Throat, Brow, Crown

Tektite
Star Signs: Aries, Cancer
Chakra: Crown

Thulite
Star Signs: Taurus, Gemini
Chakra: Heart

Tibetan Quartz
Star Sign: All
Chakra: All

Tiffany Stone
Star Sign: Aries
Chakra: Heart

Tiger's Eye
Star Sign: Capricorn
Chakra: Solar Plexus

Tiger Iron
Star Sign: Leo
Chakra: Base

Tinguaite
Star Sign: None
Chakra: None

Titanium Quartz
Star Signs: All
Chakras: All

Topaz
Star Sign: Sagittarius
Chakras: Sacral, Solar Plexus

Tourmaline
Star Sign: Libra
Chakras: All

Tourmalinated Quartz
Star Signs: All
Chakras: All

Tree Agate
Star Sign: Taurus
Chakra: Heart

Tremolite
Star Sign: None
Chakra: None

Trigonic Quartz
Star Sign: None
Chakra: None

Trummer Jasper
Star Sign: None
Chakra: None

Tugtupite
Star Signs: Taurus, Libra
Chakra: Heart

Tugtupite with Nuummite
Star Sign: Leo
Chakra: Crown

Turquoise
Star Signs: Scorpio, Sagittarius
Chakra: Throat

U

Ulexite
Star Sign: Gemini
Chakras: Brow, Crown

Unakite
Star Sign: Scorpio
Chakra: Heart

Uvarovite Garnet
Star Sign: Aquarius
Chakra: Heart

Uvite Tourmaline on Magnesite
Star Sign: None
Chakra: None

V

Valentine
Star Sign: None
Chakra: None

Vanadinite
Star Sign: Virgo
Chakra: Sacral

Variscite
Star Signs: Taurus, Gemini
Chakra: Heart

Vera Cruz Amethyst
Star Sign: Pisces
Chakras: Crown, Brow

Verdelite
Star Sign: Capricorn
Chakras: Heart, Brow

Vivianite
Star Sign: Capricorn
Chakras: Heart, Brow

Vogesite
Star Sign: None
Chakra: None

W

Watermelon Tourmaline
Star Signs: Gemini, Virgo
Chakra: Heart

White Calcite
Star Sign: Cancer
Chakra: Crown

White Sapphire
Star Signs: Virgo, Libra
Chakra:s Brow, Crown

Winchite
Star Sign: None
Chakra: None

Wind Fossil Agate
Star Sign: None
Chakra: All

Wonder Stone
Star Sign: None
Chakra: None

Wulfenite
Star Sign: Sagittarius
Chakra: Heart

X

Xenotime
Star Sign: None
Chakra: None

Y

Yellow Apatite
Star Sign: Gemini
Chakras: Throat, Solar Plexus

Yellow Crackle Quartz
Star Sign: None
Chakra: None

Yellow Fluorite
Star Sign: Leo
Chakra: Sacral

Yellow Jasper
Star Sign: Leo
Chakra: Solar Plexus

Yellow Labradorite
Star Signs: Leo, Scorpio
Chakras: Solar Plexus, Brow

Yellow Sapphire
Star Sign: Leo
Chakras: Brow, Crown

Yellow Smithsonite
Star Signs: Virgo, Pisces
Chakra: Heart

Yellow Scapolite
Star Sign: Taurus
Chakra: Brow

Yellow Spinel
Star Signs: Aries, Sagittarius
Chakras: Base, Solar Plexus

Yellow Topaz
Star Signs: Sagittarius, Leo
Chakra: Sacral

Yellow Tourmaline
Star Sign: Leo
Chakra: Solar Plexus

Yttrian Fluorite
Star Sign: Pisces
Chakras: Heart, Brow

Youngite
Star Sign: None
Chakra: Solar Plexus

Z

Zebra Stone
Star Signs: Taurus, Gemini
Chakra: Sacral

Zincite
Star Signs: Taurus, Libra
Chakras: Base, Sacral

Zircon
Star Signs: Leo, Virgo
Chakra: Base

Zoisite
Star Sign: Gemini
Chakra: Heart

Index

Page numbers in **bold** refer to main uses, and in *italics* to the A–Z of Crystals.